Better Homes and Gardens®

chicken

COOKING FOR TODAY

BETTER HOMES AND GARDENS® BOOKS

Des Moines

BETTER HOMES AND GARDENS® BOOKS
An Imprint of Meredith® Books
President, Book Group: Joseph J. Ward
Vice President and Editorial Director: Elizabeth P. Rice
Executive Editor: Connie Schrader
Art Director: Ernest Shelton
Art Production: Randall Yontz
Graphic Production Coordinator: Paula Forest
Test Kitchen Director: Sharon Stilwell

CHICKEN
Writer: Patricia A. Ward
Editor: Mary Major Williams
Graphic Designer: Tom Wegner
Test Kitchen Product Supervisor: Marilyn Cornelius
Food Stylists: Lynn Blanchard, Janet Pittman, Jennifer Peterson
Photographers: Mike Dieter, Scott Little
Cover Photographer: Andy Lyons

Meredith Corporation Corporate Officers:
Chairman of the Executive Committee: E. T. Meredith III
Chairman of the Board, President and Chief Executive Officer: Jack D. Rehm
Group Presidents: Joseph J. Ward, Books; William T. Kerr, Magazines; Philip A. Jones, Broadcasting;
    Allen L. Sabbag, Real Estate
Vice Presidents: Leo R. Armatis, Corporate Relations; Thomas G. Fisher, General Counsel and Secretary;
    Larry D. Hartsook, Finance; Michael A. Sell, Treasurer; Kathleen J. Zehr, Controller and Assistant Secretary

WE CARE!

All of us at Better Homes and Gardens® Books are dedicated to providing you with the information
and ideas you need to create tasty foods. We welcome your comments and suggestions. Write us at:
Better Homes and Gardens® Books, Cookbook Editorial Department, RW-240, 1716 Locust St.,
Des Moines, IA 50309-3023

If you would like to order additional copies of any of our books,
call 1-800-678-2803 or check with your local bookstore.

Our seal assures you that every recipe in *Chicken* has been
tested in the Better Homes and Gardens® Test Kitchen.
This means that each recipe is practical and reliable, and
meets our high standards of taste appeal. We guarantee
your satisfaction with this book for as long as you own it.

Chicken is so versatile. You can grill, fry, stew, stir-fry, roast, or bake it. That's why we divided the 68 recipes in this book into sections based on various cooking methods. There are comforting stews and oven options that cook to perfection leaving you time to prepare other menu items. If you're looking for the convenience of range-top cooking, check the first chapter with its company-pleasing Citrus Chicken and an updated Country Captain. Get out your wok for Oriental-style cooking, with a variety of seasonings and flavors in the Sizzling Stir-Fries chapter. Enjoy summertime eating year-round with grilled chicken recipes. For the more traditional, try the roasted birds that are anything but conventional. The last two chapters feature superb salads and sandwiches to round out the collection.

CONTENTS

CHICKEN BUYING AND STORAGE GUIDE

■ Chicken like other fresh meats is perishable and should be purchased and stored carefully to maintain top quality.

■ Check the "sell by" date on the package label. This is the last day the product should be sold. Chicken will retain its freshness for a few days after this date if properly refrigerated.

■ Refrigerate raw chicken promptly after purchase. Never leave chicken in a hot car or on a countertop at room temperature. You can store chicken for 1 to 2 days in your refrigerator.

■ Packaged raw chicken can be refrigerated in the original wrapping in the coldest part of refrigerator.

■ Freeze raw chicken if not used in two days (see Freezing and Thawing Tips).

■ Never leave cooked chicken at room temperature for more than 2 hours.

■ If cooked chicken is stuffed, always remove stuffing and refrigerate meat and stuffing in separate containers.

■ Store cooked chicken for picnics or box lunches in an insulated container or ice chest.

WHEN IS CHICKEN DONE?

■ Whole Roasted Chicken is done when the thickest part of the meat near the bone is no longer pink, the juices run clear, the drumsticks twist easily in their sockets, and a meat thermometer inserted in the thickest part of the thigh registers 180° to 185° (white meat should read 170°).

■ Bone-in Chicken Parts are done when you can insert a cooking fork into the chicken easily and the juices run clear. When you cut chicken with a knife, it will be no longer pink.

■ Boneless Chicken Pieces are done when the center is no longer pink. Cut chicken with a knife to check if no longer pink.

FREEZING AND THAWING TIPS

■ Remove raw chicken from the original package. Wrap chicken in heavy duty foil or plastic wrap or store in a large plastic freezer bag. Press air out of package before sealing and label with date and contents.

■ Cooked chicken should be prepared for freezing as above. If chicken is prepared with sauce or gravy, pack into a rigid plastic container with a tight-fitting lid.

■ Always defrost frozen chicken in the refrigerator or in the microwave, never, never on the kitchen counter. Bacteria multiply rapidly at room temperature.

POULTRY HOTLINE

For answers to your questions about chicken handling or safety, call the U.S. Department of Agriculture's Meat and Poultry Hotline. The toll-free number is (800) 535-4555. (In the Washington, D.C., area, call 447-3333.) Home economists at the hot line take calls from 10 a.m. to 4 p.m. eastern time.

NUTRITION FACTS

■ Chicken is lower in calories and fat than most meats. A three-ounce serving of roasted chicken breast without skin has less than 120 calories and contains just 4 grams of saturated fat.

■ We included Nutrition Information per Serving for each recipe in this book. In addition to the number of calories per serving, you'll find the amount of protein, carbohydrates, fat (includes amount of saturated fat), cholesterol, sodium and potassium.

In determining the amounts of these nutrients per serving, we assumed the following:

■ Garnishes and optional ingredients were omitted from the nutritional analysis.

■ Ingredients with a weight or amount range (¼ to ½ teaspoon, for example), were analyzed at the lesser weight or amount.

■ Where you find two ingredient options to pick from (cilantro or parsley, for example), the first was used in the nutritional rundown.

QUICK-COOKED CHICKEN

If you need cooked chicken for a recipe but don't have any leftovers, try one of these timesaving options.

■ For 2 cups cubed, cooked chicken, start with ¾ pound boneless, skinless chicken breasts.

■ Poaching: In a large skillet place chicken and 1½ cups water. Bring to boiling; reduce heat. Cover and simmer for 12 to 14 minutes or till chicken is tender and no longer pink. Drain well.

■ Micro-cooking: Arrange chicken breasts in an 8x8x2-inch baking dish, tucking under thin portions. Cover with vented clear plastic wrap. Micro-cook on 100 percent power (HIGH) for 8 to 11 minutes or till chicken is tender and no longer pink, rearranging pieces after 4 minutes. (This timing is for 600- to 700-watt countertop microwave ovens and is approximate because ovens vary.)

■ Cut up cooked chicken. Cover and chill for 2 hours or till thoroughly chilled. Or, quick-chill the chicken by putting it in the freezer for 30 minutes.

CHICKEN HANDLING TIPS

For best quality and safety, use these tips when preparing chicken.

■ Wash your hands, utensils, and work surfaces with hot, soapy water after handling raw chicken to prevent spreading bacteria to other foods.

■ Cut raw chicken on an acrylic cutting board instead of a wooden one. Porous wooden boards are difficult to wash thoroughly.

■ Rinse and pat chicken dry with paper towels before cooking.

■ When grilling chicken, keep it refrigerated until time to cook. Never place grilled chicken on same plate used to take raw chicken to the grill.

■ Always marinate chicken in the refrigerator.

■ Reheat leftovers to bubbling (about 185°) for the best taste and food safety.

COUNTRY CAPTAIN CHICKEN

Reduce the fat in your favorite recipes by skinning the chicken and skipping the browning step as we did when we updated this Georgia classic. Just the right blend of seasonings gives this version the flavor of the original recipe with a fraction of the calories.

2½ to 3 pounds meaty chicken pieces (breasts, thighs, and drumsticks)
1 14½-ounce can chunky-style stewed tomatoes
¼ cup snipped parsley
¼ cup currants *or* raisins
1 tablespoon curry powder
½ teaspoon instant chicken bouillon granules
½ teaspoon ground mace *or* nutmeg
¼ teaspoon sugar
1 tablespoon cornstarch
1 tablespoon cold water
Hot cooked rice
2 tablespoons toasted slivered almonds (optional)

Skin chicken. Rinse chicken; pat dry with paper towels. In a large skillet stir together *undrained* tomatoes, parsley, currants or raisins, curry powder, bouillon granules, mace or nutmeg, and sugar. Place chicken in skillet. Spoon tomato mixture over chicken. Bring to boiling; reduce heat. Cover and simmer for 35 to 45 minutes or till chicken is tender and no longer pink. Using a slotted spoon, remove chicken from the skillet; keep warm.

For sauce, skim fat from tomato mixture in skillet. In a small mixing bowl stir together cornstarch and cold water; add to skillet. Cook and stir till thickened and bubbly. Cook and stir for 2 minutes more. Serve chicken and sauce with rice. Sprinkle with almonds, if desired. Makes 6 servings.

Nutrition information per serving: 394 calories, 32 g protein, 40 g carbohydrate, 11 g fat (3 g saturated), 86 mg cholesterol, 276 mg sodium, 515 mg potassium.

CITRUS CHICKEN

Grab your skillet and this recipe when you need a quick meal for guests. To complete the meal, toss mixed greens with a light vinaigrette and end with a citrus-flavored sorbet.

4   medium skinless, boneless chicken
      breast halves (about 12 ounces
      total)
2   teaspoons finely shredded orange peel
1   cup orange juice
¼   cup balsamic vinegar *or* white wine
      vinegar
1   tablespoon cornstarch
2   teaspoons honey
1   teaspoon instant chicken bouillon
      granules
      Dash white pepper
2   cups sliced fresh shiitake *or* button
      mushrooms
2   tablespoons margarine *or* butter
8   ounces tomato linguine *and/or* plain
      linguine, cooked
      Snipped chives (optional)
      Orange slices, halved (optional)

Rinse chicken; pat dry with paper towels. Place each breast half between 2 pieces of plastic wrap. Working from center to the edges, pound lightly with the flat side of a meat mallet to ⅛-inch thickness. Remove plastic wrap.

In small bowl stir together the orange peel, orange juice, vinegar, cornstarch, honey, bouillon granules, and pepper. Set aside.

In a large skillet cook mushrooms in hot margarine or butter till tender; remove from skillet. In the same skillet cook chicken over medium heat about 4 minutes or till no longer pink, turning once. Remove chicken from skillet; keep warm. Return mushrooms to skillet. Stir orange juice mixture; add to mushrooms. Cook and stir till thickened and bubbly. Cook and stir for 2 minutes more. Serve chicken and sauce over linguine. Sprinkle with chives and garnish with orange slices, if desired. Makes 4 servings.

Nutrition information per serving: 434 calories, 25 g protein, 62 g carbohydrate, 9 g fat (2 g saturated), 45 mg cholesterol, 329 mg sodium, 348 mg potassium.

OLIVE CHICKEN

Another quick skillet entrée that's perfect for company. Serve a side of steamed whole green beans and an accompanying salad made of arugula, toasted pecans, and strips of red sweet pepper.

2½ **to 3 pounds meaty chicken pieces (breasts, thighs, and drumsticks)**
1 **tablespoon olive oil *or* cooking oil**
1 **medium onion, finely chopped**
1 **small carrot, finely chopped**
2 **to 3 tablespoons snipped Italian *or* curly-leaf parsley**
2 **cloves garlic, minced**
1 **teaspoon dried sage, crushed**
¼ **teaspoon pepper**
½ **cup chicken broth**
½ **cup dry white wine**
2 **tablespoons tomato paste**
1 **teaspoon cornstarch**
1 **tablespoon cold water**
⅓ **cup sliced pitted ripe olives *or* Italian black olives in brine**
⅓ **cup sliced pitted green olives**

Skin chicken. Rinse chicken; pat dry with paper towels. In a large skillet cook chicken in hot oil over medium heat for 10 to 15 minutes or till chicken is lightly browned, turning to brown evenly. Remove chicken; set aside.

Add the onion, carrot, parsley, garlic, sage, and pepper to skillet; cook for 4 to 5 minutes or till vegetables are tender. Stir in chicken broth, wine, and tomato paste. Return chicken to skillet. Spoon sauce over chicken. Bring to boiling; reduce heat. Cover and simmer for 20 minutes. Uncover; cook for 5 to 10 minutes more or till chicken is tender and no longer pink. Remove chicken from the skillet; keep warm.

For sauce, skim fat from the mixture in skillet. In small bowl stir together cornstarch and water; add to skillet. Cook and stir till thickened and bubbly. Stir in sliced olives; cook and stir for 2 minutes more. To serve, spoon sauce over chicken. Makes 6 servings.

Nutrition information per serving: 331 calories, 30 g protein, 11 g carbohydrate, 17 g fat (4 g saturated), 86 mg cholesterol, 797 mg sodium, 471 mg potassium.

CHICKEN WITH PEAS AND POTATOES

Save clean-up time with this chicken meal-in-a-skillet featuring tiny red-skinned potatoes and peas in a rosemary-scented sauce.

1   2½- to 3-pound cut up broiler-fryer
      chicken *or* 2 pounds chicken thighs
1   pound small new potatoes, quartered
2   tablespoons margarine *or* butter
¾   cup chicken broth
1   teaspoon dried rosemary, crushed
¼   teaspoon pepper
4   green onions, thinly sliced
1   10-ounce package frozen peas
¼   cup snipped parsley
1   8-ounce carton dairy sour cream
2   tablespoons all-purpose flour
      Snipped parsley (optional)

Skin chicken, if desired. Rinse and pat dry with paper towels. Scrub potatoes. If desired, remove a narrow strip of peel from the center of each potato.

In a 12-inch skillet cook chicken in hot margarine or butter over medium heat about 15 minutes or till chicken is browned, turning to brown evenly. Add potatoes, broth, rosemary, and pepper. Bring to boiling; reduce heat. Cover and simmer for 30 minutes.

Add green onions, peas, and ¼ cup parsley to skillet. Cover and simmer about 10 minutes more or till the chicken and potatoes are tender and chicken is no longer pink. Using a slotted spoon, transfer chicken and vegetables to platter; keep warm.

Remove skillet from heat. Stir together sour cream and flour; stir into broth in skillet. Cook and stir till thickened and bubbly; cook and stir for 1 minute more. Spoon sauce over chicken and vegetables; sprinkle with additional parsley, if desired. Makes 6 servings.

Nutrition information per serving: 491 calories, 34 g protein, 28 g carbohydrate, 27 g fat (10 g saturated), 106 mg cholesterol, 286 mg sodium, 703 mg potassium.

QUICK CHICKEN MOLE

Continue the Mexican theme by serving warm flour tortillas, tomato salsa seasoned with chopped cilantro, and sliced oranges layered with coconut for dessert.

6   medium chicken breast halves
        (about 2¼ pounds total)
2   tablespoons olive oil *or* cooking oil
1   small onion, chopped
1   clove garlic, minced
1½   teaspoons chili powder
1   teaspoon sesame seed
¼   teaspoon ground cumin
¼   teaspoon ground cinnamon
¼   teaspoon salt
1   small tomato, chopped
1   tomatilla, peeled and cut into wedges
        or 1 small tomato, chopped
½   cup chicken broth
½   cup tomato sauce
2   tablespoons raisins
2   teaspoons unsweetened cocoa powder
     Several dashes bottled hot pepper
        sauce
     Hot cooked rice
     Toasted pumpkin seeds *or* slivered
        almonds (optional)

Skin chicken. Rinse chicken; pat dry with paper towels. In a large skillet cook chicken in hot oil over medium heat about 10 minutes or till chicken is lightly browned, turning to brown evenly. Add onion, garlic, chili powder, sesame seed, cumin, cinnamon, and salt. Cook and stir for 30 seconds.

Stir in tomato, tomatilla, chicken broth, tomato sauce, raisins, cocoa powder, and hot pepper sauce. Bring to boiling; reduce heat. Simmer, uncovered, about 15 minutes or till chicken is tender and no longer pink. Using a slotted spoon, remove chicken. Simmer sauce to reduce to desired consistency (4 to 5 minutes).

To serve, spoon sauce over chicken and rice. Sprinkle with pumpkin seeds or almonds, if desired. Makes 6 servings.

Nutrition information per serving: 367 calories, 33 g protein, 37 g carbohydrate, 9 g fat (2 g saturated), 76 mg cholesterol, 543 mg sodium, 572 mg potassium.

BUFFALO CHICKEN DRUMSTICKS

Here's a drumstick version of the popular chicken wing recipe. If you like a little less fire, use 2 tablespoons hot pepper sauce and add 1 teaspoon vinegar for flavor.

8 medium chicken drumsticks (about 2 pounds total)
2 tablespoons all-purpose flour
½ teaspoon paprika
2 tablespoons cooking oil
½ cup chopped onion
1 clove garlic, minced
½ cup chicken broth
2 to 4 tablespoons bottled hot pepper sauce
  Celery sticks
¼ cup blue cheese salad dressing

Skin chicken, if desired. Rinse chicken; pat dry with paper towels. In a plastic or paper bag combine flour and paprika. Add chicken, a few pieces at a time, shaking to coat well. In a 10-inch skillet cook chicken in hot oil over medium heat about 10 minutes or till chicken is lightly browned, turning to brown evenly. Remove chicken; set aside.

In drippings in skillet cook onion and garlic about 5 minutes or till golden brown and tender. Combine chicken broth and hot pepper sauce; stir into skillet. (Avoid inhaling fumes caused by cooking the hot pepper sauce.) Return chicken to skillet. Bring to boiling; reduce heat. Cover and simmer about 15 minutes or till chicken is tender and no longer pink.

Transfer chicken to platter. Skim fat from sauce, if necessary. To serve, spoon some of the sauce over chicken; pass remaining sauce. Serve with celery sticks and blue cheese dressing. Makes 4 servings.

Nutrition information per serving: 444 calories, 32 g protein, 11 g carbohydrate, 30 g fat (7 g saturated), 112 mg cholesterol, 488 mg sodium, 644 mg potassium.

CHICKEN AND VEGETABLE SKILLET

Try this combination another time with angel hair pasta and a sprinkle of freshly grated Parmesan cheese.

1   2½- to 3-pound cut up broiler-fryer
    chicken,
¼   cup all-purpose flour
½   teaspoon paprika
½   teaspoon salt
¼   teaspoon pepper
2   tablespoons cooking oil
½   cup chopped onion
2   cloves garlic, minced
1   tablespoon grated gingerroot
¾   cup chicken broth
1   pound fresh asparagus, cut into
    1-inch pieces
2   red *or* green sweet peppers, cut into
    1-inch strips
3   yellow summer squash *and/or*
    zucchini, cut into 1-inch chunks
8   ounces fresh mushrooms, thickly
    sliced (3 cups)
¼   cup dry sherry
2   tablespoons soy sauce
2   teaspoons cornstarch
    Hot cooked orzo, rice, *or* noodles

Skin chicken, if desired. Rinse chicken; pat dry with paper towels. In a plastic or paper bag combine flour, paprika, salt, and pepper. Add chicken, a few pieces at a time, shaking to coat well.

In a 12-inch skillet cook chicken in hot oil over medium heat about 10 minutes or till chicken is lightly browned, turning to brown evenly. Remove chicken; set aside. If necessary, add 1 tablespoon additional oil.

Add the onion, garlic, and gingerroot to skillet; cook for 4 to 5 minutes or till onion is tender. Carefully stir in chicken broth. Return chicken to skillet. Bring to boiling; reduce heat. Cover and simmer about 15 minutes or till chicken is tender and no longer pink. Spoon off excess fat.

Add the asparagus, sweet peppers, squash, and mushrooms. In a measuring cup combine dry sherry, soy sauce, and cornstarch; stir to mix. Stir into skillet. Return to boiling; reduce heat. Cover and simmer about 5 to 10 minutes more or till vegetables are crisp-tender. Serve with orzo, rice and noodles. Makes 4 to 6 servings.

Nutrition information per serving: 621 calories, 51 g protein, 33 g carbohydrate, 31 g fat (7 g saturated), 134 mg cholesterol, 1,069 mg sodium, 1,115 mg potassium.

CHICKEN BREASTS WITH CORN SAUCE

Complete this home-style meal with steamed broccoli spears and garnish with fresh lemon wedges.

6   medium chicken breast halves
      (about 2¼ pounds total)
1   tablespoon snipped fresh basil *or*
      1 teaspoon dried basil, crushed
½   teaspoon ground nutmeg
¼   teaspoon pepper
3   tablespoons cooking oil
4   green onions, sliced
1   8-ounce carton dairy sour cream
2   tablespoons all-purpose flour
⅔   cup milk
1   7-ounce can whole kernel corn with
      sweet peppers, drained
2   tablespoons snipped parsley

Skin chicken, if desired. Rinse chicken; pat dry with paper towels. In a small bowl combine basil, nutmeg, and pepper. Brush chicken with *1 tablespoon* of the oil. Rub basil mixture over chicken.

In a 12-inch skillet cook chicken in remaining oil over medium heat about 10 minutes or till chicken is browned, turning once.

Sprinkle chicken with green onions. Reduce heat. Cover and cook about 30 minutes or till chicken is tender and no longer pink.

Meanwhile, in a small bowl stir together sour cream and flour; gradually stir in milk. Remove chicken from skillet. Drain fat. Add the sour cream mixture to the skillet. Cook and stir till thickened and bubbly. Stir in corn. Return chicken to skillet and heat through. Spoon sauce onto six plates; top each with a chicken breast. Sprinkle with parsley before serving. Makes 6 servings.

Nutrition information per serving: 350 calories, 31 g protein, 10 g carbohydrate, 21 g fat (8 g saturated), 97 mg cholesterol, 100 mg sodium, 394 mg potassium.

SPINACH FETTUCCINE WITH CHICKEN

Although packaged grated Parmesan can be used here, we find that freshly grated or shredded cheese intensifies the flavor. If you use a food processor, you'll have all the cheese you'll need in no time.

6 ounces spinach fettuccine *or* plain
   fettuccine
4 ounces fresh mushrooms, sliced
¼ cup sliced green onions
2 tablespoons margarine *or* butter
2 tablespoons all-purpose flour
¼ teaspoon salt
¼ teaspoon coarsely ground pepper
¼ teaspoon ground nutmeg
1½ cups milk
½ cup grated *or* finely shredded
   Parmesan cheese
2 tablespoons dry sherry
2 cups cubed cooked chicken
   (10 ounces)
½ cup sliced pitted ripe olives
   Snipped chives (optional)
   Lemon wedges (optional)

Cook fettuccine according to package directions. Drain well.

Meanwhile, in a 12-inch skillet cook mushrooms and green onions in margarine or butter about 5 minutes or till vegetables are tender. Stir in flour, salt, pepper, and nutmeg. Add milk; cook and stir until thickened and bubbly. Cook and stir for 1 minute more. Add *half* of the Parmesan cheese and the sherry; heat until cheese is melted.

Add fettuccine, chicken, and ripe olives to skillet. Toss lightly to coat. Sprinkle with remaining Parmesan and, if desired, chives. Serve with lemon wedges, if desired. Makes 4 servings.

Nutrition information per serving: 506 calories, 37 g protein, 42 g carbohydrate, 20 g fat (7 g saturated), 84 mg cholesterol, 639 mg sodium, 535 mg potassium.

CHICKEN PAPRIKA

For more flavor, we suggest the Hungarian paprika—it comes in both hot and sweet versions.

8   ounces fresh mushrooms, sliced
      (3 cups)
1   medium onion, chopped (½ cup)
2   cloves garlic, minced
¼   cup margarine *or* butter
2   to 3 teaspoons Hungarian paprika *or*
      paprika
¼   teaspoon pepper
2   cups cubed cooked chicken
      (10 ounces)
1   14½-ounce can chicken broth
2   tablespoons tomato paste
1   8-ounce carton dairy sour cream *or*
      reduced-calorie dairy sour cream
3   tablespoons all-purpose flour
      Hot cooked wide noodles
      Snipped parsley (optional)

In a 10-inch skillet cook mushrooms, onion, and garlic in melted margarine or butter over medium heat about 5 minutes or till vegetables are tender. Stir in paprika and pepper. Cook and stir for 1 minute more. Stir in cubed cooked chicken, chicken broth, and tomato paste. Bring to boiling.

Stir together sour cream and flour. Stir into mixture in skillet. Cook and stir till thickened and bubbly. Cook and stir for 1 minute more. Serve chicken mixture over noodles. Garnish with snipped parsley, if desired. Makes 4 servings.

Nutrition information per serving: 542 calories, 32 g protein, 33 g carbohydrate, 31 g fat (11 g saturated), 119 mg cholesterol, 592 mg sodium, 751 mg potassium.

SWEET AND SOUR CHICKEN

Our recipe testers noted that this recipe takes a bit more time to prepare than most in this book, but is well worth the effort.

1	**pound skinless, boneless chicken breasts** *or* **thighs**
1	**beaten egg**
1	**cup packaged biscuit mix**
⅓	**cup water**
1½	**cups cooking oil**
1	**20-ounce can pineapple chunks (juice pack)**
⅓	**cup sugar**
¼	**cup soy sauce**
¼	**cup cider vinegar**
2	**tablespoons cornstarch**
2	**teaspoons paprika**
1	**tablespoon cooking oil**
1	**large green sweet pepper, cut lengthwise into strips**
4	**green onions, cut into 2-inch lengths**
2	**cups cherry tomatoes, halved**
	Hot cooked rice

Rinse chicken; pat dry with paper towels. Cut chicken into 1-inch pieces. In a medium bowl combine egg, biscuit mix and water. Dip chicken pieces into batter to coat.

Heat 1½ cups cooking oil in wok or small deep-fat fryer over medium heat (375°). Fry chicken pieces in hot oil, a few at a time, until golden brown (about 2 minutes). Remove chicken pieces as they brown and drain on paper towels. Discard cooking oil. Keep chicken warm in a 300° oven.

For sauce, drain pineapple, reserving juice. Add enough water to juice to make 1¾ cups. In a bowl combine sugar, soy sauce, vinegar, cornstarch, and paprika. Add pineapple juice mixture; set aside.

Add 1 tablespoon cooking oil to wok or 12-inch skillet. Preheat over medium-high heat. Stir-fry green sweet pepper and green onions in hot oil for 2 to 3 minutes or till crisp-tender. Remove vegetables from wok. Stir sauce; add to center of wok. Cook and stir till slightly thickened and bubbly. Add cooked vegetables, pineapple chunks, and tomatoes to wok. Cook and stir about 2 minutes more or till heated through. Add chicken; stir to coat. Serve immediately over cooked rice. Makes 6 servings.

Nutrition information per serving: 482 calories, 20 g protein, 60 g carbohydrate, 19 g fat (3 g saturated), 75 mg cholesterol, 843 mg sodium, 528 mg potassium.

PACIFIC RIM STIR-FRY

Adjust the hotness of this stir-fry by reducing or increasing the amount of chili oil used.

 3 ounces rice sticks (also called rice
    noodles) *or* thin vermicelli, broken
12 ounces skinless, boneless chicken
    thighs *or* breasts
 ½ cup chicken broth
 2 tablespoons soy sauce
 2 tablespoons snipped fresh basil *or*
    2 teaspoons dried basil, crushed
 2 teaspoons cornstarch
 1 teaspoon chili oil *or* ½ teaspoon
    crushed red pepper
 ½ teaspoon ground turmeric
 1 tablespoon cooking oil
 2 medium carrots, cut into julienne
    strips
 2 cups broccoli flowerets
 1 red *or* green sweet pepper, cut into
    1-inch strips (½ cup)
 ¼ cup cashew halves *or* peanuts

In a saucepan cook rice sticks in boiling water for 3 minutes. (Or, cook vermicelli according to package directions.) Drain. Set aside; keep warm.

Meanwhile, rinse chicken; pat dry with paper towels. Cut chicken thighs or breasts into thin, bite-sized strips; set aside.

For sauce, combine chicken broth, soy sauce, basil, cornstarch, chili oil or crushed red pepper, and turmeric; set aside.

Add cooking oil to wok or 12-inch skillet. Preheat over medium-high heat (add more oil if necessary during cooking). Stir-fry carrot strips in hot oil for 1 minute. Add broccoli flowerets; stir-fry for 2 minutes more. Add red or green sweet pepper strips; stir-fry for 1½ to 3 minutes more or till crisp-tender. Remove vegetables from wok. Add chicken to wok; stir-fry for 2 to 3 minutes or till no longer pink. Push chicken from center of wok.

Stir sauce; add to center of wok. Cook and stir till thickened and bubbly. Return vegetables to wok. Stir to coat. Cook and stir 2 minutes more or till heated through. Serve immediately over hot rice sticks or vermicelli. Top with cashews or peanuts. Makes 4 servings.

Nutrition information per serving: 309 calories, 17 g protein, 32 g carbohydrate, 13 g fat (3 g saturated), 41 mg cholesterol, 748 mg sodium, 539 mg potassium.

CURRIED CHICKEN THIGHS

You can also use skinless, boneless chicken thighs in this recipe. Just reduce the cooking time to 10 minutes after adding chicken broth.

8 chicken thighs (about 2½ pounds total)
2 tablespoons cooking oil
1 cup sliced fresh mushrooms
1 medium onion, chopped (½ cup)
1 clove garlic, minced
3 to 4 teaspoons curry powder
¼ teaspoon salt
¼ teaspoon ground cinnamon
¾ cup chicken broth
1 medium apple, cored and chopped
1 cup half-and-half, light cream, *or* milk
2 tablespoons all-purpose flour
3 cups hot cooked rice
Assorted condiments: raisins, chopped hard-cooked egg, peanuts, chopped tomato, chopped green sweet pepper, toasted coconut, chutney, cut-up fruits (optional)

Skin chicken. Rinse chicken; pat dry with paper towels. In a 10-inch skillet cook chicken thighs in hot oil over medium heat about 10 minutes or till chicken is lightly browned, turning to brown evenly. Remove chicken; set aside. If necessary, add 1 tablespoon additional cooking oil to skillet.

Add mushrooms, onion, and garlic to skillet; cook till vegetables are tender. Add curry powder, salt, and cinnamon; cook and stir for 1 minute. Add chicken broth and chopped apple. Return chicken to skillet. Bring to boiling; reduce heat. Cover and simmer about 15 minutes or till chicken is tender and no longer pink.

Transfer chicken to platter; keep warm. Stir the half-and-half, light cream, *or* milk into the flour. Stir into pan juices. Cook and stir till thickened and bubbly. Cook and stir for 1 minute more. Spoon some sauce over chicken. Pass remaining sauce. Serve with rice and, if desired, pass assorted condiments. Makes 4 servings.

Nutrition information per serving: 695 calories, 54 g protein, 45 g carbohydrate, 32 g fat (10 g saturated), 158 mg cholesterol, 829 mg sodium, 718 mg potassium.

PEKING CHICKEN STIR-FRY

Look for the wonton wrappers next to the produce in your supermarket or any Oriental grocery store.

12 dried shiitake mushrooms
12 ounces skinless, boneless chicken
      breasts *or* thighs
½ cup chicken broth
2 tablespoons soy sauce
2 tablespoons dry sherry
2 teaspoons cornstarch
¼ to ½ teaspoon chili oil *or* chili paste
2 tablespoons peanut oil *or* cooking oil
1 tablespoon grated gingerroot
2 cloves garlic, minced
1 carrot, thinly sliced (½ cup)
3 stalks celery, cut into thin diagonal
      slices (1½ cups)
1 red *or* green sweet pepper, cut into
      lengthwise strips (¾ cup)
2 green onions, cut into 2-inch lengths
      (¼ cup)
½ of a medium bok choy, coarsely
      chopped (4 cups)
1½ cups pea pods, strings removed and
      cut in diagonal halves
1 14-ounce can baby corn, drained
      Hot cooked rice *or* Fried Wonton
      Strips

In a small bowl place shiitake mushrooms. Add boiling water to cover; let soak for 30 minutes. Drain; trim and discard the stems. Cut caps into halves. Set aside.

Meanwhile, rinse chicken; pat dry with paper towels. Cut chicken into bite-sized strips; set aside. For sauce, stir together chicken broth, soy sauce, sherry, cornstarch, and chili oil or paste; set aside.

Add peanut or cooking oil to a wok or 12-inch skillet. Preheat over medium-high heat (add more oil if necessary during cooking). Stir-fry gingerroot and garlic in hot oil for 15 seconds. Add carrot; stir-fry for 1 minute. Add celery; stir-fry for 1 minute. Add red or green sweet pepper and green onions; stir-fry for 1 to 2 minutes more or till vegetables are crisp-tender. Remove vegetables and set aside.

Add bok choy to wok or skillet. Stir-fry for 2 minutes. Add pea pods and reserved mushrooms; stir-fry for 1 to 2 minutes more or till crisp-tender. Remove vegetables from wok and set aside.

Add chicken to wok; stir-fry for 2 to 3 minutes or till no longer pink. Push chicken from center of wok. Stir sauce; add to center of wok. Cook and stir till thickened and bubbly. Return all of the cooked vegetables to wok. Add corn. Stir to coat. Cook and stir about 1 minute more or till heated through. Serve immediately over cooked rice or Fried Wonton Strips. Makes 4 servings.

Fried Wonton Strips: Cut 15 wonton wrappers into ¼-inch strips. Carefully drop several at a time into deep hot oil (365°). Fry for about 30 seconds or till crisp and golden. Remove with slotted spoon. Drain on paper towels.

Nutrition information per serving: 456 calories, 29 g protein, 58 g carbohydrate, 11 g fat (2 g saturated), 45 mg cholesterol, 386 mg sodium, 1,591 mg potassium.

SESAME CHICKEN AND VEGETABLES

To make the garnish, cut a 3-inch length of green onion and then cut green part into narrow strips. Chill in iced water a few minutes so it curls.

12   ounces skinless, boneless chicken
       breasts
 2   tablespoons soy sauce
 2   tablespoons chicken broth
 2   tablespoons chopped green onion
 1   tablespoon snipped parsley
 1   tablespoon rice vinegar
1½ teaspoons sesame seed
 1   clove garlic, minced
1½ teaspoons grated gingerroot
 1   tablespoon sesame oil
1½ cups thinly bias-sliced carrots
 1   cup jicama cut into thin, bite-sized
       strips
 6   ounces fresh medium pea pods,
       strings removed, *or* one 6-ounce
       package frozen pea pods
       Hot cooked brown rice

Rinse chicken; pat dry with paper towels. Cut chicken into bite-sized strips. For marinade, in a shallow nonmetallic dish combine soy sauce, chicken broth, green onion, parsley, rice vinegar, sesame seed, garlic, and gingerroot. Add chicken to marinade, stirring to coat. Cover and chill for 1 hour.

Add 1 tablespoon sesame oil to wok or 12-inch skillet. Preheat over medium-high heat (add more oil if necessary during cooking). Stir-fry carrots in hot oil for 1 minute. Add jicama and fresh pea pods (if using); stir-fry about 2 to 3 minutes more or till crisp-tender. Remove vegetables from wok. Drain chicken, reserving marinade. Add chicken to wok; stir-fry for 2 to 3 minutes or till no longer pink. Push chicken from center of wok.

Add reserved marinade to center of wok. Cook and stir till bubbly. Return cooked vegetables to wok. Add frozen pea pods (if using). Stir to coat. Cook and stir about 1 minute more or till heated through. Serve immediately over hot cooked brown rice, spooning sauce over top. Makes 4 servings.

Nutrition information per serving: 304 calories, 22 g protein, 37 g carbohydrate, 8 g fat (1 g saturated), 45 mg cholesterol, 621 mg sodium, 414 mg potassium.

ASIAN NOODLES WITH CHICKEN STIR-FRY

Reduce calories from fat by serving this stir-fry over steamed white rice or Chinese egg noodles instead of the fried bean threads.

3	cups peanut oil
2	ounces bean thread vermicelli
12	ounces skinless, boneless chicken breasts *or* thighs
¾	cup chicken broth
2	tablespoons teriyaki sauce
4	teaspoons cornstarch
1	tablespoon cooking oil
2	tablespoons finely chopped lemongrass *or* 1 teaspoon finely shredded lemon peel
2	cloves garlic, minced
2	cups broccoli flowerets
1	cup cauliflower flowerets
4	ounces fresh shiitake mushrooms, stems removed and sliced
1	red *or* green sweet pepper, cut into 1-inch squares
8	green onions, cut into 2-inch lengths
2	medium tomatoes, cut into wedges
	Snipped cilantro *or* parsley (optional)

In a wok or 12-inch skillet heat the 3 cups of peanut oil to 375°. Add the vermicelli to hot oil and cook about 8 seconds or till puffed, turning once. (Do not let brown.) Drain on paper towels; set aside. Discard peanut oil.

Rinse chicken; pat dry with paper towels. Cut chicken into 1-inch pieces; set aside.

For sauce, in a small bowl combine chicken broth, teriyaki sauce, and cornstarch; set aside.

Add 1 tablespoon cooking oil to the same wok or a 12-inch skillet. Preheat over medium-high heat (add more oil if necessary during cooking). Stir-fry lemongrass or lemon peel and garlic in hot oil for 15 seconds. Add the broccoli and cauliflower; stir-fry for 2 minutes. Add the mushrooms, red or green sweet pepper, and green onions; stir-fry for 1½ to 2 minutes more or till vegetables are crisp-tender. Remove vegetables from wok. Add chicken to wok; stir-fry about 4 minutes or till no longer pink. Push chicken from center of wok.

Stir sauce; add to center of wok. Cook and stir until thickened and bubbly. Return cooked vegetables to wok. Add tomatoes. Stir to coat. Cook and stir about 2 minutes more or till heated through. Serve immediately with vermicelli. Sprinkle with cilantro or parsley, if desired. Makes 4 servings.

Nutrition information per serving: 386 calories, 24 g protein, 30 g carbohydrate, 20 g fat (4 g saturated), 45 mg cholesterol, 658 mg sodium, 784 mg potassium.

HOT AND SPICY CHICKEN WITH PEANUTS AND LEEKS

Cut the heat in this dish by omitting the dried chili peppers and using the lesser amount of hot pepper sauce.

1   **pound skinless, boneless chicken thighs *or* breasts**
⅓   **cup water**
2   **tablespoons soy sauce**
2   **tablespoons dry sherry**
2   **teaspoons cornstarch**
½   **to ¾ teaspoon bottled hot pepper sauce**
1   **tablespoon cooking oil**
2   **cloves garlic, minced**
2   **teaspoons grated gingerroot**
3   **leeks, cleaned and cut into 2-inch strips (½ cup)**
6   **whole small dried red chili peppers (optional)**
½   **cup peanuts**
    Hot cooked rice

Rinse chicken; pat dry with paper towels. Cut chicken into bite-size strips; set aside.

For sauce, in a small bowl combine water, soy sauce, dry sherry, cornstarch, and hot pepper sauce; set aside.

Add oil to wok or 12-inch skillet. Preheat over medium-high heat (add more oil if necessary during cooking). Stir-fry garlic and ginger-root in hot oil for 15 seconds. Add leeks and, if desired, chili peppers. Stir-fry for 1½ minutes or till leeks are crisp-tender. Remove leek mixture from wok. Add half of the chicken to wok. Stir-fry for 2 to 3 minutes or till no longer pink. Remove chicken from wok. Repeat with remaining chicken. Return all chicken to wok; push chicken from center of wok.

Stir sauce; add to center of wok. Cook and stir till thickened and bubbly. Return cooked vegetables to wok. Stir to coat. Cook and stir about 1 minute more or till heated through. Stir in peanuts. Serve immediately over cooked rice. Makes 4 servings.

Nutrition information per serving: 396 calories, 24 g protein, 32 g carbohydrate, 19 g fat (3 g saturated), 54 mg cholesterol, 583 mg sodium, 378 mg potassium.

CHICKEN-MUSHROOM LO MEIN

Enjoy lo mein at home without calling the Chinese take-out--it's easy and tastes terrific.

12 ounces skinless, boneless chicken
    breasts *or* thighs
2 tablespoons soy sauce
2 tablespoons dry sherry
2 teaspoons cornstarch
8 ounces linguine
1 tablespoon cooking oil
1 tablespoon toasted sesame oil
8 ounces fresh mushrooms, sliced
    (3 cups)
1 medium red *or* green sweet pepper,
    cut into 2-inch strips (1 cup)
4 green onions, cut into 2-inch pieces
6 ounces fresh pea pods, strings
    removed (1½ cups)
½ cup water
¼ teaspoon instant chicken bouillon
    granules

Rinse chicken; pat dry with paper towels. Cut chicken into thin, bite-sized strips. In a small bowl stir together soy sauce, dry sherry, and cornstarch. Add chicken; stir to coat. Cover and chill for 30 minutes.

Meanwhile, cook linguine according to package directions, omitting oil and salt. Drain well.

Add cooking oil and sesame oil to a wok or 12-inch skillet. Preheat over medium-high heat (add more oil if necessary during cooking). Add mushrooms, red or green sweet peppers, and green onions to wok; stir-fry for 2 minutes. Add pea pods and stir-fry about 1 minute more or till vegetables are crisp-tender. Remove vegetables from wok.

Drain chicken, reserving liquid. Stir-fry chicken for 2 to 3 minutes or till no longer pink. Combine water, bouillon granules, and reserved marinade; add to wok. Cook and stir till thickened and bubbly. Add drained linguine and cooked vegetables. Stir to coat. Cook and stir about 1 minute more or till heated through. Makes 4 servings.

Nutrition information per serving: 434 calories, 28 g protein, 54 g carbohydrate, 11 g fat (2 g saturated), 45 mg cholesterol, 616 mg sodium, 532 mg potassium.

CHICKEN WITH FRESH PINEAPPLE

Add to the tropical feel of this Asian-style dish by garnishing with wedges of fresh pineapple.

12 **ounces skinless, boneless chicken thighs *or* breasts**
⅓ **cup unsweetened pineapple juice**
¼ **cup orange juice**
1½ **teaspoons cornstarch**
¼ **teaspoon crushed red pepper**
1 **tablespoon cooking oil**
2 **cloves garlic, minced**
1 **medium green sweet pepper, cut into 1-inch squares (1 cup)**
4 **green onions, cut into 2-inch pieces**
½ **medium pineapple, peeled, cored, and cut into 1-inch chunks (1½ cups)**
Hot cooked rice
¼ **cup coarsely chopped cashews**

Rinse chicken; pat dry with paper towels. Cut chicken into thin, bite-sized strips. Set aside.

For sauce, in a small bowl combine pineapple juice, orange juice, cornstarch, and crushed red pepper. Set aside.

Add oil to wok or 12-inch skillet. Preheat over medium-high heat (add more oil if necessary during cooking). Stir-fry garlic in hot oil for 15 seconds. Add green sweet pepper and green onions. Stir-fry for 1½ minutes. Remove vegetables from the wok.

Add chicken to wok. Stir-fry chicken for 2 to 3 minutes or till no longer pink. Push chicken from center of wok. Stir sauce; add to center of wok. Cook and stir until thickened and bubbly. Return cooked vegetables to wok. Add pineapple. Stir to coat. Cook and stir about 1 minute more or till heated through. Serve immediately over cooked rice. Sprinkle with cashews. Makes 4 servings.

Nutrition information per serving: 359 calories, 21 g protein, 45 g carbohydrate, 10 g fat (2 g saturated), 45 mg cholesterol, 96 mg sodium, 383 mg potassium.

BROCCOLI CHICKEN STIR-FRY

Using shredded lettuce instead of rice adds a pleasant crispness and lightness to this stir-fry.

12 ounces skinless, boneless chicken
    breasts
1 pound broccoli
½ cup chicken broth
2 tablespoons teriyaki sauce
2 teaspoons cornstarch
1 teaspoon toasted sesame oil
2 to 3 tablespoons cooking oil
1 tablespoon grated gingerroot
1 clove garlic, minced
2 cups fresh medium mushrooms,
    halved *or* quartered
8 ounces fresh bean sprouts (2 cups)
1 red *or* green sweet pepper, cut into
    lengthwise strips (¾ cup)
1 8-ounce can sliced water chestnuts,
    drained
4 cups coarsely shredded lettuce
    (optional)

Rinse chicken; pat dry with paper towels. Cut chicken into 1-inch pieces. Set aside. Remove flowerets from broccoli and cut in half (you should have about 3½ cups). Cut stalks into 1½-inch lengths and then into ¼-inch strips (you should have about 1½ cups); set aside.

For sauce, in a small bowl combine chicken broth, teriyaki sauce, cornstarch, and sesame oil; set aside.

Add 2 tablespoons cooking oil to a wok or 12-inch skillet. Preheat over medium-high heat (add more oil if necessary during cooking). Stir-fry gingerroot and garlic in hot oil for 10 seconds. Add broccoli stems; stir-fry for 1 minute. Add broccoli flowerets; stir-fry for 2 to 3 minutes or till crisp-tender. Remove broccoli from wok. Add mushrooms to wok; stir-fry about 1½ minutes or till crisp-tender. Remove from wok. Add bean sprouts and red or green sweet pepper to wok; stir-fry for 1 to 2 minutes or till crisp-tender. Remove from wok. Add chicken to wok. Stir-fry for 4 to 5 minutes or till no longer pink. Push chicken from center of wok.

Stir sauce; add to center of wok. Cook and stir until thickened and bubbly. Return cooked vegetables to wok. Add water chestnuts. Stir to coat. Cook and stir about 2 minutes more or till heated through. Serve immediately over shredded lettuce, if desired. Makes 4 servings.

Nutrition information per serving: 261 calories, 24 g protein, 19 g carbohydrate, 11 g fat (2 g saturated), 45 mg cholesterol, 524 mg sodium, 869 mg potassium.

CHICKEN AND VEGETABLE STEW

Hearty stews, particularly this rosemary-seasoned one, are rewarding comfort food year-round.

8 small chicken thighs (about 2 pounds total)
2 tablespoons cooking oil
2 cups water
8 small new potatoes, halved
4 medium carrots, sliced into 1-inch pieces (2 cups)
2 stalks celery, bias sliced into ¾-inch pieces (1 cup)
1 cup fresh green beans cut into 1½-inch pieces *or* frozen cut green beans
1 small onion, chopped (⅓ cup)
2 tablespoons tomato paste
1 bay leaf
¾ teaspoon salt
½ teaspoon dried rosemary, crushed
1 medium zucchini, quartered lengthwise and cut into ½-inch slices (1¼ cups)
¼ cup cold water
2 tablespoons all-purpose flour
   Snipped parsley (optional)

Skin chicken. Rinse chicken; pat dry with paper towels. In a 4½-quart Dutch oven cook chicken in hot oil over medium heat for 10 to 15 minutes or till chicken is lightly browned, turning to brown evenly. Drain fat.

Add 2 cups water, potatoes, carrots, celery, fresh green beans (if using), onion, tomato paste, bay leaf, salt, and rosemary. Bring to boiling. Reduce heat; cover and simmer for 25 minutes.

Add zucchini and frozen green beans (if using). Cook, covered, for 10 to 15 minutes more or till chicken is tender and no longer pink. Discard bay leaf.

Combine ¼ cup water and flour. Add to chicken mixture. Cook and stir until thickened and bubbly. Cook and stir for 1 minute more. Sprinkle with parsley, if desired. Makes 4 servings.

Nutrition information per serving: 424 calories, 31 g protein, 43 g carbohydrate, 15 g fat (4 g saturated), 93 mg cholesterol, 581 mg sodium, 1,188 mg potassium.

CINCINNATI-STYLE CHICKEN CHILI

Freshly shredded Romano cheese adds a flavor boost to this Midwestern favorite.

1   pound ground raw chicken
1   large onion, chopped
1   clove garlic, minced
3   tablespoons chili powder
2   teaspoons paprika
1   teaspoon ground cumin
½   teaspoon salt
½   teaspoon ground cinnamon
⅛   teaspoon ground cloves
⅛   teaspoon ground red pepper
1   bay leaf
1   14½-ounce can stewed tomatoes
1   8-ounce can tomato sauce
½   cup water
1   tablespoon red wine vinegar
1   tablespoon molasses
1   15½-ounce can kidney beans
    Hot cooked spaghetti

In a 4 1/2-quart Dutch oven cook ground chicken, onion, and garlic over medium heat for 5 to 7 minutes or till chicken is no longer pink. Drain fat, if necessary.

Add chili powder, paprika, cumin, salt, cinnamon, cloves, red pepper, and bay leaf. Cook and stir over medium heat for 3 minutes more. Stir in *undrained* stewed tomatoes, tomato sauce, water, vinegar, and molasses. Bring to boiling. Reduce heat; cover and simmer for 45 minutes, stirring occasionally.

Uncover and simmer to desired consistency. Discard bay leaf. In a medium saucepan heat kidney beans; drain. To serve, spoon sauce and beans over hot spaghetti. Makes 4 servings.

Nutrition information per serving: 402 calories, 30 g protein, 61 g carbohydrate, 8 g fat (2 g saturated), 54 mg cholesterol, 1,223 mg sodium, 1,145 mg potassium.

CHICKEN RATATOUILLE

The chicken simmers to perfection in this excellent vegetable combination that originated in the Mediterranean.

1   2½- to 3-pound cut up broiler-fryer
      chicken, cut up
2   tablespoons cooking oil
1   large onion, sliced
1   clove garlic, minced
2   large tomatoes, diced
1   large green sweet pepper, cut into
      ½-inch strips
1   small eggplant (about 1 pound),
      peeled and cut into 1-inch chunks
2   small zucchini, cut into ½-inch chunks
1   bay leaf
½   teaspoon salt
¼   teaspoon pepper
3   slices bacon, crisp-cooked, drained,
      and crumbled
    Snipped parsley (optional)

Skin chicken. Rinse chicken; pat dry with paper towels. In a 4½-quart Dutch oven cook chicken in hot oil over medium heat about 10 minutes or till chicken is lightly browned, turning to brown evenly. Remove chicken; set aside.

Add onion and garlic to drippings in Dutch oven. Cook about 5 minutes or till tender. Add tomatoes, green sweet pepper, eggplant, zucchini, bay leaf, salt, and pepper. Return chicken to Dutch oven. Bring to boiling; reduce heat. Cover and simmer about 30 minutes or till chicken is tender and no longer pink, stirring occasionally. Spoon off excess fat, if necessary.

Stir in bacon. Discard bay leaf. If desired, for a thicker sauce, transfer chicken to serving bowl; keep warm. Simmer vegetables, uncovered, for 5 to 10 minutes more. Pour sauce over chicken. Sprinkle with parsley before serving, if desired. Makes 6 servings.

Nutrition information per serving: 339 calories, 31 g protein, 12 g carbohydrate, 19 g fat (5 g saturated), 92 mg cholesterol, 313 mg sodium, 630 mg potassium.

CHICKEN VEGETABLE RAGOUT

Mop up the thick, well-seasoned sauce with some crusty French bread.

2 **pounds meaty chicken pieces (breasts, thighs, and drumsticks)**
2 **tablespoons cooking oil**
1 **large onion, chopped (1 cup)**
8 **ounces fresh mushrooms, quartered**
2 **cloves garlic, minced**
1 **tablespoon snipped fresh thyme** *or* **1 teaspoon dried thyme, crushed**
½ **teaspoon pepper**
¼ **teaspoon salt**
1 **bay leaf**
2 **cups chicken broth**
½ **cup dry white wine**
4 **medium carrots, cut into 1-inch chunks**
4 **parsnips, peeled and cut into 1-inch chunks**
⅓ **cup chicken broth**
3 **tablespoons all-purpose flour**
Snipped parsley (optional)

Skin chicken. Rinse chicken; pat dry with paper towels. In a 4½-quart Dutch oven cook chicken over medium heat in hot oil for 10 to 15 minutes or till chicken is lightly browned, turning to brown evenly. Remove chicken; set aside.

Add the onion, mushrooms, garlic, thyme, pepper, salt, and bay leaf to Dutch oven; cook for 4 to 5 minutes or till vegetables are tender. Carefully stir in 2 cups chicken broth and the white wine. Add carrots and parsnips. Return chicken to Dutch oven. Bring to boiling; reduce heat. Cover and simmer for 30 to 35 minutes or till chicken is tender and no longer pink and vegetables are tender.

Using a slotted spoon, transfer chicken and vegetables to a serving dish; keep warm. If necessary, spoon excess fat from broth mixture in Dutch oven. Discard bay leaf. Combine ⅓ cup chicken broth and the flour. Stir into broth mixture. Cook and stir till thickened and bubbly; cook and stir for 1 minute more. Spoon sauce over chicken and vegetables. Garnish with parsley, if desired. Makes 4 servings.

Nutrition information per serving: 466 calories, 40 g protein, 32 g carbohydrate, 18 g fat (4 g saturated), 104 mg cholesterol, 769 mg sodium, 1,087 mg potassium.

CHICKEN WITH BASIL AND BEANS

A good beverage choice for this chicken dish is chilled light beer or iced tea

2½ to 3 pounds meaty chicken pieces
      (breasts, thighs, and drumsticks)
1 medium onion, chopped (½ cup)
1 clove garlic, minced
1 tablespoon cooking oil
1 14½-ounce can Italian-style plum
      tomatoes, cut up
1 tablespoon snipped fresh basil *or*
      1 teaspoon dried basil, crushed
1 tablespoon snipped fresh oregano *or*
      1 teaspoon dried oregano, crushed
½ teaspoon coarsely ground pepper
¼ teaspoon salt
1 15-ounce can butter beans, rinsed and
      drained
1 8-ounce can red kidney beans, rinsed
      and drained

Skin chicken. Rinse chicken; pat dry with paper towels. Set aside.

In a 4½-quart Dutch oven cook onion and garlic in hot oil over medium heat till onion is tender. Add *undrained* tomatoes, basil, oregano, pepper, and salt. Add chicken. Bring mixture to boiling. Reduce heat. Cover and simmer about 45 minutes or till chicken is tender and no longer pink.

Transfer chicken to a serving platter; keep warm. Stir butter beans and kidney beans into Dutch oven; return to boiling. Simmer, uncovered, for 5 minutes more. Spoon bean mixture over chicken. Makes 6 servings.

Nutrition information per serving: 253 calories, 27 g protein, 21 g carbohydrate, 8 g fat (2 g saturated), 61 mg cholesterol, 468 mg sodium, 575 mg potassium.

CHICKEN AND MUSHROOMS IN RED WINE

Special enough for guests. Accompany with sautéed zucchini slices and garnish with a sprig of fresh rosemary.

4 small chicken legs (drumstick-thigh
    piece) (about 2 pounds total)
2 tablespoons all-purpose flour
¾ teaspoon garlic salt
¼ teaspoon pepper
2 tablespoons cooking oil
½ cup dry red wine
½ cup chicken broth
16 pearl onions (1⅓ cups)
2 cups fresh medium mushrooms,
    quartered
2 tablespoons tomato paste
1½ teaspoons snipped fresh rosemary *or*
    ½ teaspoon dried rosemary, crushed
1½ teaspoons snipped fresh thyme *or*
    ½ teaspoon dried thyme, crushed
1 bay leaf
2 tablespoons chicken broth
1 tablespoon all-purpose flour
6 slices bacon, crisp-cooked, drained,
    and crumbled
    Snipped parsley (optional)
    Hot cooked noodles

Skin chicken. Rinse chicken; pat dry with paper towels. In a plastic or paper bag combine 2 tablespoons flour, garlic salt, and pepper. Add chicken, one or two pieces at a time, to the bag, shaking to coat chicken well.

In a 4½-quart Dutch oven cook chicken in hot oil about 10 minutes or till lightly browned, turning to brown evenly. Drain. Add wine, ½ cup chicken broth, onions, mushrooms, tomato paste, rosemary, thyme, and bay leaf. Bring to boiling; reduce heat. Cover and simmer for 35 to 40 minutes or till chicken is tender and no longer pink. Discard bay leaf. Transfer chicken to a platter; keep warm.

Stir together 2 tablespoons broth and 1 tablespoon flour. Add to mushroom mixture in Dutch oven. Cook and stir till thickened and bubbly. Cook and stir for 1 minute more. Stir in bacon. Spoon some of the mushroom sauce over chicken; sprinkle with parsley, if desired. Pass remaining sauce. Serve with hot noodles. Makes 4 servings.

Nutrition information per serving: 468 calories, 37 g protein, 35 g carbohydrate, 18 g fat (4 g saturated), 122 mg cholesterol, 764 mg sodium, 790 mg potassium.

CHICKEN WITH APRICOTS AND PRUNES

Boost the flavor in the rice accompaniment with toasted slivered almonds and snipped parsley.

2   to 2½ pounds meaty chicken pieces
         (breasts, thighs, and drumsticks)
½   teaspoon garlic powder
½   teaspoon salt
¼   teaspoon pepper
2   tablespoons cooking oil
1   6-ounce package dried apricots, cut
         into halves
1   cup pitted prunes, cut into halves
1   cup chicken broth
¾   cup dry white wine
¼   cup white wine vinegar
1   tablespoon brown sugar
3   inches stick cinnamon
4   whole cloves
3   tablespoons water
3   tablespoons Dijon-style mustard
4   teaspoons all-purpose flour
     Chopped green onion (optional)
     Hot cooked rice

Skin chicken, if desired. Rinse chicken; pat dry with paper towels. Season with garlic powder, salt, and pepper.

In a 4½-quart Dutch oven cook chicken in hot oil over medium heat about 15 minutes or till chicken is lightly browned, turning to brown evenly. Drain off fat.

Add apricots, prunes, chicken broth, white wine, wine vinegar, brown sugar, stick cinnamon, and whole cloves. Bring to boiling. Reduce heat; cover and simmer for 35 to 40 minutes or till chicken is tender and no longer pink.

Using a slotted spoon, transfer chicken and fruit to a platter; keep warm. Discard stick cinnamon and cloves. For sauce, in a small bowl stir together water, mustard, and flour. Stir flour mixture into cooking liquid. Cook and stir till thickened and bubbly. Cook and stir for 1 minute more. Spoon some of the sauce over chicken and fruit. Pass remaining sauce. Garnish with chopped green onion, if desired. Serve with cooked rice. Makes 6 servings.

Nutrition information per serving: 570 calories, 29 g protein, 82 g carbohydrate, 13 g fat (3 g saturated), 69 mg cholesterol, 580 mg sodium, 943 mg potassium.

SPICY CHICKEN WITH BEANS

If you prefer, use red kidney beans instead of the black beans in this spicy main dish.

1   pound ground raw chicken
1   large onion, chopped (1 cup)
2   cloves garlic, minced
1   tablespoon cooking oil
1   teaspoon ground cumin
½   teaspoon salt
½   teaspoon pepper
1   28-ounce can tomatoes, cut up
1   15-ounce can tomato sauce
4   pickled jalapeño peppers, seeded and
    chopped (optional)
1   15-ounce can black beans, rinsed and
    drained
1   15-ounce can great northern beans,
    rinsed and drained
¼   dairy sour cream *or* shredded cheddar
    cheese
    Sliced green onion (optional)

In a large saucepan cook chicken, onion, and garlic in hot oil over medium heat for 8 to 10 minutes or till chicken is no longer pink and onion is tender. Drain off fat.

Add cumin, salt, and pepper; cook and stir for 1 minute more. Stir in *undrained* tomatoes, tomato sauce, and, if desired, jalapeño peppers. Bring to boiling. Reduce heat; cover and simmer for 20 minutes, stirring occasionally. Add black beans and great northern beans; heat through. Serve topped with sour cream or cheese and, if desired, sliced green onion. Makes 4 to 6 servings.

Nutrition information per serving: 438 calories, 34 g protein, 54 g carbohydrate, 13 g fat (4 g saturated), 60 mg cholesterol, 1,251 mg sodium, 1,360 mg potassium.

HEARTY MIDWESTERN CHICKEN AND NOODLES

Chicken legs are often a good buy, and in this hearty dish, turn rather ordinary vegetables into a comforting home-style dinner.

3 chicken legs (drumstick-thigh piece)
   (about 2 pounds)
4 cups water
½ cup chopped celery leaves
2 tablespoons snipped parsley
1 bay leaf
1 teaspoon dried thyme, crushed
1 teaspoon salt
¼ teaspoon pepper
1½ cups chopped onion
2 cups sliced carrots
1 cup sliced celery
3 cups wide noodles
1 cup loose-pack frozen peas
2 cups milk
2 tablespoons all-purpose flour

Skin chicken. Rinse chicken; pat dry with paper towels. In a 4½-quart Dutch oven place chicken, water, celery leaves, parsley, bay leaf, thyme, salt, and pepper. Heat to boiling. Reduce heat. Cover and simmer for 30 minutes.

Add the onion, carrots, and sliced celery. Cover and simmer about 30 minutes more or till chicken is tender and no longer pink. Remove from heat. Remove chicken; cool slightly. Discard the bay leaf. Remove meat from bones; discard bones. Chop chicken and set aside.

Heat vegetable mixture to boiling. Add noodles; cook for 5 minutes. Stir in peas and *1½ cups* of the milk.

In a screw-top jar combine remaining milk and flour. Cover and shake until smooth. Stir into noodle mixture. Cook and stir till thickened and bubbly. Stir in chicken. Cook for 1 to 2 minutes more or till heated through. Makes 6 servings.

Nutrition information per serving: 321 calories, 24 g protein, 38 g carbohydrate, 8 g fat (2 g saturated), 83 mg cholesterol, 535 mg sodium, 589 mg potassium.

WISCONSIN CHEESE-STUFFED CHICKEN ROLLS

Cook your family's favorite rice combo and sugar snap peas for a meal that's anything but ordinary.

2 tablespoons dried tomatoes
   (not oil pack)
4 medium skinless, boneless chicken
   breast halves (about 12 ounces
   total)
2 tablespoons all-purpose flour
¼ teaspoon salt
⅛ teaspoon pepper
⅓ cup fine dry bread crumbs
2 tablespoons grated Parmesan cheese
½ teaspoon paprika
1 egg
4 ounces sharp cheddar cheese
½ to 1 teaspoon dried fines herbes *or*
   leaf sage, crushed
1 tablespoon margarine *or* butter,
   melted

In small bowl place dried tomatoes. Add enough boiling water to cover; soak for 10 minutes. Drain and pat dry with paper towels. Finely chop; set aside.

Rinse chicken; pat dry with paper towels. Place each breast half between 2 pieces of plastic wrap. Working from center to the edges, pound lightly with the flat side of a meat mallet to ⅛-inch thickness. Remove plastic wrap.

In a small shallow bowl combine the flour, salt, and pepper. In another small shallow bowl combine the bread crumbs, Parmesan cheese, and paprika. In another small bowl slightly beat the egg.

Cut cheddar cheese into four 3x1x½-inch pieces. Place a cheese stick on each pounded chicken breast half. Sprinkle each with some of the chopped dried tomatoes and dried herbs. Fold in the sides of each chicken breast and roll up tightly. Roll in flour mixture, egg, and then bread crumb mixture.

Arrange chicken rolls, seam side down, in a 2-quart rectangular baking dish. (To make ahead, cover and chill for 1 to 4 hours.) Drizzle chicken rolls with melted margarine or butter. Bake, uncovered, in a 350° oven for 20 to 25 minutes or till chicken is tender and no longer pink. Makes 4 servings.

Nutrition information per serving: 317 calories, 28 g protein, 11 g carbohydrate, 17 g fat (8 g saturated), 130 mg cholesterol, 953 mg sodium, 272 mg potassium.

OVEN-FRIED CHICKEN

For a fresh-tasting accompaniment, sprinkle sliced tomatoes with basil and marinate in a light salad dressing while chicken is baking.

1　beaten egg
3　tablespoons milk
1　cup finely crushed saltine crackers
　　(about 28)
1　teaspoon dried thyme, crushed
½　teaspoon paprika
⅛　teaspoon pepper
2½　to 3 pounds meaty chicken pieces
　　(breasts, thighs, and drumsticks)
2　tablespoons margarine *or* butter,
　　melted

In a small bowl combine the egg and the milk. In a shallow dish combine the crackers, thyme, paprika, and pepper. Set aside.

Skin chicken. Rinse chicken; pat dry with paper towels. Dip chicken pieces, one at a time, in egg mixture, then roll in cracker mixture.

In a greased 15x10x1-inch or 13x9x2-inch baking pan arrange chicken so the pieces don't touch. Drizzle chicken pieces with melted margarine or butter.

Bake in a 375° oven for 45 to 55 minutes or till the chicken pieces are tender and no longer pink. *Do not* turn the chicken pieces while baking. Makes 6 servings.

Nutrition information per serving: 253 calories, 24 g protein, 10 g carbohydrate, 12 g fat (3 g saturated), 105 mg cholesterol, 296 mg sodium, 247 mg potassium.

TANDOORI-STYLE CHICKEN

Ordinary chicken takes on an Indian flair in this easy-to-do dish.

1 2½- to 3-pound cut-up broiler-fryer
  chicken
1 8-ounce carton plain low-fat yogurt
2 tablespoons lemon juice
1 tablespoon grated gingerroot *or*
   1 teaspoon ground ginger
1 tablespoon cooking oil
2 cloves garlic, minced
2 teaspoons chili powder
1 to 2 teaspoons ground cumin
1 teaspoon paprika
½ teaspoon salt
½ teaspoon ground turmeric

Skin chicken. Rinse chicken; pat dry with paper towels. Place chicken pieces in a 2-quart rectangular baking dish.

For sauce, in a small bowl stir together yogurt, lemon juice, gingerroot, cooking oil, garlic, chili powder, cumin, paprika, salt, and turmeric. Spoon sauce atop chicken. Cover and chill for 2 to 24 hours, turning occasionally.

Bake, uncovered, in a 375° oven for 25 minutes. Spoon juices over chicken and bake for 25 minutes more or till chicken is tender and no longer pink. Transfer chicken to a platter (discard pan juices). Makes 4 to 6 servings.

Nutrition information per serving: 352 calories, 45 g protein, 7 g carbohydrate, 15 g fat (4 g saturated), 132 mg cholesterol, 446 mg sodium, 556 mg potassium.

SWEET AND TANGY BARBECUED CHICKEN

Oven meals make cooking easy--add some baking potatoes to the oven while the chicken bakes and follow up with an apple crisp.

1   medium onion, chopped (½ cup)
1   clove garlic, minced
1   tablespoon cooking oil
1   8-ounce can tomato sauce
½   cup packed brown sugar
½   cup cider vinegar
2   tablespoons Dijon-style mustard
1   teaspoon dried thyme, crushed
½   teaspoon pepper
6   chicken legs (thigh-drumstick piece)
      (about 3½ pounds total)

For sauce, in a 1½-quart saucepan cook onion and garlic in hot oil till tender. Stir in tomato sauce, brown sugar, vinegar, Dijon-style mustard, thyme, and pepper. Bring to boiling; reduce heat. Simmer, uncovered, for 15 minutes, stirring occasionally. (Sauce can be made ahead; cover and chill till needed.)

Skin chicken, if desired. Rinse chicken; pat dry with paper towels. Arrange chicken in a 15x10x1-inch baking pan. Pour *half* of the sauce over chicken.

Bake, uncovered, in a 375° oven for 50 to 60 minutes or till chicken is tender and no longer pink, basting occasionally with additional sauce. Serve chicken with any remaining sauce. Makes 6 servings.

Nutrition information per serving: 420 calories, 35 g protein, 24 g carbohydrate, 20 g fat (5 g saturated), 120 mg cholesterol, 493 mg sodium, 561 mg potassium.

BAKED CHICKEN IN RED PEPPER SAUCE

Here's an easy oven recipes that you can prepare without fuss. Meaty chicken pieces are baked with a tangy-sweet red pepper sauce

¼   cup all-purpose flour
½   teaspoon salt
½   teaspoon paprika
¼   teaspoon pepper
2   to 2½ pounds meaty chicken pieces
       (breasts, thighs, and drumsticks)
2   tablespoons margarine *or* butter,
       melted
1   medium red *or* green sweet pepper,
       cut into squares
¼   cup sliced green onion
1   tablespoon cooking oil
2   tablespoons all-purpose flour
1   cup chicken broth
2   tablespoons sugar
¼   to ½ teaspoon crushed red pepper
⅓   cup cider vinegar

In a plastic or paper bag combine the ¼ cup flour, salt, paprika, and pepper.

Skin chicken. Rinse chicken; pat dry with paper towels. Add chicken, a few pieces at a time, to the bag, shaking to coat well. Arrange chicken in a shallow baking pan; drizzle with melted margarine or butter. Bake in a 375° oven for 30 minutes.

Meanwhile, for sauce, in a medium saucepan, cook red or green sweet pepper and green onion in hot oil till tender. Stir in 2 tablespoons flour. Add chicken broth, sugar, and crushed red pepper. Cook and stir until thickened and bubbly. Cook and stir for 1 minute more. Remove from heat; stir in vinegar and cool slightly.

Spoon sauce over chicken. Bake for 30 minutes more or till chicken is tender and no longer pink, basting with sauce two or three times during baking. Reheat any remaining sauce and pass with chicken. Makes 6 servings.

Nutrition information per serving: 213 calories, 18 g protein, 12 g carbohydrate, 10 g fat (2 g saturated), 49 mg cholesterol, 397 mg sodium, 225 mg potassium.

HONEYED CHICKEN

For a zippy appetizer use this glaze for 10 to 12 chicken wings. Cut the wings at the joints and discard the wing tips or reserve them for another use. Makes about 20 appetizers.

8 **chicken drumsticks *and/or* thighs**
   (about 2 pounds total)
¼ **cup finely chopped green onion**
¼ **cup honey**
¼ **teaspoon garlic powder**
   Dash ground red pepper

Rinse chicken; pat dry with paper towels. Arrange chicken pieces in a 15x10x1-inch baking pan making sure pieces do not touch. Bake in a 400° oven for 30 minutes.

Meanwhile, combine green onion, honey, garlic powder, and ground red pepper. Brush chicken pieces with honey mixture. Return to oven. Bake for 15 to 20 minutes more or till golden brown and chicken is no longer pink. Makes 4 servings.

Nutrition information per serving: 327 calories, 29 g protein, 17 g carbohydrate, 15 g fat (4 g saturated), 103 mg cholesterol, 98 mg sodium, 271 mg potassium.

CHICKEN WITH SAFFRON RICE

Here's a simple version of a Spanish paella traditionally named after the utensil it's cooked in—
a two-handled pan that also serves as a casserole.

6   small chicken breast halves *or*
        6 medium thighs (about 2 pounds
        total)
2   tablespoons cooking oil
1   medium onion, chopped (½ cup)
2   cloves garlic, minced
1   cup long grain rice
1   6½-ounce can minced clams
1   teaspoon ground cumin
½   teaspoon salt
¼   teaspoon pepper
⅛   teaspoon ground saffron *or*
        ¼ teaspoon thread saffron
1   14½-ounce can stewed tomatoes
1   14½-ounce can chicken broth
¼   cup water
1   10-ounce package frozen peas
8   ounces medium raw shrimp, shelled
        and deveined
½   cup sliced pitted ripe olives
        Parsley sprigs (optional)

Rinse chicken; pat dry with paper towels. In a 12-inch ovenproof skillet, cook chicken in hot oil over medium heat about 10 minutes or till chicken is lightly browned, turning to brown evenly. Remove chicken.

Add onion and garlic to skillet. Cook about 5 minutes or till onion is tender. Stir in rice. Cook and stir till rice is light brown.

Drain clams, reserving liquid; set aside. Stir cumin, salt, pepper, and saffron into skillet; add *undrained* stewed tomatoes, chicken broth, water, and reserved clam liquid. Bring to boiling. Top with chicken pieces. Cover tightly and bake in a 400° oven for 15 minutes.

Stir in reserved clams, peas, shrimp, and olives. Cover and bake about 15 minutes more or till chicken is tender and no longer pink and shrimp turn pink. Let stand 5 minutes before serving. Garnish with parsley, if desired. Makes 6 servings.

Nutrition information per serving: 437 calories, 41 g protein, 42 g carbohydrate, 12 g fat (3 g saturated), 145 mg cholesterol, 893 mg sodium, 733 mg potassium.

CREAMY CHICKEN AND SPAGHETTI BAKE

While it bakes, toss a green salad and heat some dinner rolls.

6	ounces spaghetti
12	ounces ground raw chicken
1	cup sliced fresh mushrooms
¼	cup chopped onion
1	clove garlic, minced
1	tablespoon cooking oil
1	tablespoon margarine *or* butter
1	tablespoon all-purpose flour
⅛	teaspoon pepper
¾	cup milk
¾	cup shredded sharp American cheese (3 ounces)
¼	cup sliced pitted ripe olives
1	tablespoon snipped parsley
1	tablespoon chopped pimiento
2	tablespoons fine dry bread crumbs
2	tablespoons grated Parmesan cheese
1	tablespoon margarine *or* butter, melted

Break spaghetti in half. Cook spaghetti according to package directions just till tender. Drain; transfer spaghetti to a large mixing bowl.

Meanwhile, in a large skillet cook chicken, mushrooms, onion, and garlic in hot oil over medium-high heat for 3 to 4 minutes or till chicken is no longer pink. Add chicken mixture to spaghetti.

For sauce, in a small saucepan melt 1 tablespoon margarine or butter. Stir in flour and pepper. Add milk all at once. Cook and stir over medium heat till thickened and bubbly. Cook and stir for 1 minute more. Add American cheese, stirring till melted. Remove from heat. Stir in olives, parsley, and pimiento.

Pour the sauce over the chicken mixture. Toss to coat. Transfer to a greased 2-quart square baking dish or casserole. In a small mixing bowl toss together bread crumbs, Parmesan cheese, and 1 tablespoon melted margarine or butter. Sprinkle over chicken mixture.

Cover and bake in a 375° oven for 20 minutes. Uncover and bake 10 to 15 minutes more or till heated through. Makes 4 servings.

Nutrition information per serving: 486 calories, 26 g protein, 41 g carbohydrate, 24 g fat (8 g saturated), 67 mg cholesterol, 611 mg sodium, 395 mg potassium.

BLUE CHEESE-STUFFED CHICKEN BREASTS

Complete the meal with steamed carrots sprinkled with parsley and a refreshing lemon sherbet for the finale.

4   large skinless, boneless chicken breast
      halves (about 1 pound total)
    Salt
    Pepper
1   3-ounce package cream cheese,
      softened
¼   cup crumbled blue cheese (1 ounce)
½   cup toasted chopped pecans
2   tablespoons margarine *or* butter,
      melted
¼   teaspoon paprika
    Snipped parsley (optional)

Rinse chicken; pat dry with paper towels. Place each breast half between 2 pieces of plastic wrap. Working from center to the edges, pound lightly with the flat side of a meat mallet to ¼-inch thickness. Remove plastic wrap. Season with salt and pepper.

In a small bowl combine cream cheese, blue cheese, and pecans. Place about ¼ cup cheese mixture on each chicken breast. Fold chicken around filling to form a mound; repeat with remaining chicken.

Place chicken portions in a 2-quart square baking dish. In a small bowl combine margarine or butter and paprika. Brush each chicken portion with mixture. Bake, uncovered, in a 350° oven about 30 minutes or till chicken is tender and no longer pink. Sprinkle with parsley, if desired. Makes 4 servings.

Nutrition information per serving: 363 calories, 26 g protein, 4 g carbohydrate, 28 g fat (9 g saturated), 88 mg cholesterol, 417 mg sodium, 288 mg potassium.

CHICKEN EGGPLANT BAKE

Lean ground chicken replaces the traditional lamb used in this rendition of the classic Greek dish, called moussaka.

1   large eggplant, peeled and sliced
      crosswise into ½-inch slices
      (1¼ pounds)
3   tablespoons olive oil *or* cooking oil
12 ounces ground raw chicken
1   medium onion, chopped (½ cup)
1   clove garlic, minced
½   teaspoon dried oregano, crushed
¼   teaspoon ground cinnamon
1   8-ounce can stewed tomatoes
2   tablespoons tomato paste
2   tablespoons margarine *or* butter
2   tablespoons all-purpose flour
1¼ cups milk
1   beaten egg
¼   cup grated Parmesan cheese
⅔   cup crumbled feta cheese (3 ounces)
      Coarsely grated *or* ground nutmeg

Place eggplant slices on broiler pan; brush surface with *1 tablespoon* of the oil. Broil 6 to 7 inches from the heat about 8 minutes or till tender, turning once and brushing with another tablespoon of oil.

Heat remaining oil in a large skillet. Cook chicken, onion, garlic, oregano, and cinnamon over medium heat about 5 minutes or till chicken is no longer pink and onion is tender. Remove from heat. Drain fat, if necessary. Stir in *undrained* stewed tomatoes and tomato paste; set aside.

For sauce, in a medium saucepan melt margarine or butter. Stir in flour. Add milk all at once. Cook and stir till thickened and bubbly. Cook and stir for 1 minute more. Gradually stir some of the sauce into the beaten egg. Then stir egg mixture back into the saucepan. Stir in Parmesan cheese.

To assemble, in a 2-quart square baking dish layer half of the eggplant, all of the meat mixture, the feta cheese, remaining eggplant slices, and all of the sauce. Sprinkle with nutmeg. Bake in a 350° oven about 30 minutes or till set. Let stand 5 minutes before serving. Makes 4 to 6 servings.

Nutrition information per serving: 447 calories, 24 g protein, 22 g carbohydrate, 30 g fat (9 g saturated), 123 mg cholesterol, 683 mg sodium, 764 mg potassium.

ALL-AMERICAN BARBECUED CHICKEN

Make it an All-American barbecue with roasted corn on the cob and macaroni salad bathed in a light vinaigrette.

1   **medium onion, finely chopped**
    (½ cup)
1   **tablespoon cooking oil**
1   **cup catsup**
½   **cup water**
¼   **cup vinegar**
2   **to 3 tablespoons brown sugar**
2   **tablespoons Worcestershire sauce**
2   **dashes bottled hot pepper sauce**
1   **2½- to 3-pound broiler-fryer chicken,**
    quartered

For sauce, in a saucepan cook onion in hot oil till onion is tender. Stir in catsup, water, vinegar, brown sugar, Worcestershire sauce, and bottled hot pepper sauce. Bring to boiling; reduce heat. Simmer, uncovered, about 15 minutes or to desired consistency.

Meanwhile, rinse chicken; pat dry with paper towels. Break wing, hip, and drumstick joints so pieces lie flat. Twist wing tips under back. Grill chicken, skin side down, on an uncovered grill directly over medium coals for 20 minutes. Turn chicken; grill for 15 to 20 minutes more or till chicken is tender and no longer pink. (*Or,* place chicken on the unheated rack of a broiler pan. Broil 5 to 6 inches from the heat for 28 to 32 minutes, turning once.) Brush with sauce during the last 10 minutes of grilling or broiling. Heat remaining sauce till bubbly; pass with chicken. Makes 4 to 6 servings.

Nutrition information per serving: 407 calories, 32 g protein, 29 g carbohydrate, 19 g fat (5 g saturated), 98 mg cholesterol, 996 mg sodium, 671 mg potassium.

TEXAS-STYLE BARBECUED CHICKEN LEGS

Cut lengthwise strips of assorted sweet peppers and grill to perfection alongside the chicken.

1 tablespoon margarine *or* butter
1 medium onion, finely chopped (½ cup)
2 cloves garlic, minced
1 teaspoon chili powder
¼ teaspoon ground sage
½ cup catsup
2 tablespoons water
2 tablespoons vinegar
1 tablespoon sugar
1 tablespoon lemon juice
1 tablespoon Worcestershire sauce
½ teaspoon salt
½ teaspoon bottled hot pepper sauce
¼ teaspoon cracked black pepper
6 chicken legs (thigh-drumstick piece)
   (about 2½ pounds total)

For sauce, in a saucepan melt margarine or butter. Add onion, garlic, chili powder, and sage. Cook and stir till onion is tender. Stir in catsup, water, vinegar, sugar, lemon juice, Worcestershire sauce, salt, bottled hot pepper sauce, and black pepper. Bring to boiling; reduce heat. Simmer, uncovered, about 5 minutes, stirring occasionally.

Meanwhile, rinse chicken; pat dry with paper towels. Grill chicken, skin side down, on an uncovered grill directly over medium coals for 20 minutes. Turn chicken; grill for 15 to 20 minutes more or till chicken is tender and no longer pink. (*Or,* place chicken on the unheated rack of a broiler pan. Broil 5 to 6 inches from the heat for 28 to 32 minutes, turning once.) Brush with sauce during the last 10 minutes of grilling or broiling. Heat remaining sauce till bubbly; pass with chicken. Makes 6 servings.

Nutrition information per serving: 276 calories, 25 g protein, 11 g carbohydrate, 15 g fat (4 g saturated), 86 mg cholesterol, 596 mg sodium, 381 mg potassium.

FOUR-SEASON GRILLED CHICKEN

Pass warm pita bread with the hot-from-the-grill chicken and finish with a refreshing pineapple sorbet garnished with mint.

1 medium onion, finely chopped (½ cup)
1 clove garlic, minced
2 tablespoons margarine *or* butter
1 teaspoon chili powder
¼ teaspoon ground cumin
¼ teaspoon ground red pepper
6 medium skinless, boneless chicken breast halves (about 1¼ pounds total)
   Shredded lettuce (optional)
   Chopped tomato (optional)
   Avocado slices (optional)

In a small saucepan cook onion and garlic in melted margarine or butter till tender. Stir in the chili powder, cumin, and ground red pepper. Cook for 1 minute. Rinse chicken; pat dry with paper towels. Brush *half* of the onion mixture over chicken.

Grill chicken on an uncovered grill directly over medium coals for 6 minutes. Turn chicken; brush with remaining onion mixture. Grill for 6 to 8 minutes more or till chicken is tender and no longer pink. (*Or*, place chicken on the unheated rack of a broiler pan. Broil 5 to 6 inches from the heat for 10 to 12 minutes, turning once and brushing with remaining onion mixture.) Serve with shredded lettuce, chopped tomato, and avocado slices, if desired. Makes 6 servings.

Nutrition information per serving: 163 calories, 22 g protein, 2 g carbohydrate, 7 g fat (2 g saturated), 59 mg cholesterol, 103 mg sodium, 208 mg potassium.

SKEWERED CHICKEN WITH PAPAYA CHUTNEY

Accompany these chicken kabobs with steamed rice spiked with dried crushed red pepper.

1   medium onion, cut into 8 wedges
1   tablespoon curry powder
2   tablespoons olive oil *or* cooking oil
2   tablespoons lemon juice
1   tablespoon water
½   teaspoon salt
¼   teaspoon pepper
1   pound skinless, boneless chicken
      breasts *or* thighs
1   red *or* green sweet pepper, cut into
      1-inch pieces
12 fresh *or* canned pineapple chunks
      Papaya Chutney

If using wooden skewers, place in water to soak.

In a small saucepan cook the onion in boiling water about 4 minutes. Drain; set aside.

Meanwhile, in a small skillet cook curry powder in hot oil for 30 seconds. Remove from heat. Add lemon juice, water, salt, and pepper; set aside.

Rinse chicken; pat dry with paper towels. Cut chicken into 1-inch cubes. On 4 long skewers thread chicken cubes, red or green sweet pepper, pineapple, and onion. Stir curry mixture; brush kabobs on all sides. Grill kabobs on an uncovered grill for 12 minutes or till chicken is tender and no longer pink, turning as needed to brown evenly. (*Or,* place kabobs on the unheated rack of a broiler pan. Broil 5 to 6 inches from the heat about 10 minutes, turning as needed.) Serve with Papaya Chutney. Makes 4 servings.

Papaya Chutney: In a medium saucepan combine 1 cup chopped, peeled *apple;* 1 cup chopped, peeled *papaya;* ¼ cup packed *brown sugar;* 2 tablespoons chopped *green sweet pepper;* 2 tablespoons *vinegar;* 2 tablespoons *raisins;* 2 tablespoons *water;* 2 teaspoons *lemon juice;* and a dash *salt.* Bring to boiling; reduce heat. Simmer, uncovered, about 15 minutes or till fruit is tender and chutney is desired consistency, stirring occasionally.

Nutrition information per serving: 337 calories, 23 g protein, 40 g carbohydrate, 11 g fat (2 g saturated), 59 mg cholesterol, 384 mg sodium, 579 mg potassium.

GRILLED LIME CHICKEN WITH PINEAPPLE SALSA

The fresh flavor of pineapple and the addition of garlic, cilantro and lime juice make this salsa perfect for either broiled or grilled chicken.

½ teaspoon finely shredded lime peel
¼ cup lime juice
1 tablespoon cooking oil
¼ teaspoon salt
¼ teaspoon coarsely ground pepper
6 medium skinless, boneless chicken
   breast halves (about 1¼ pounds
   total)
   Pineapple Salsa

Stir together lime peel, lime juice, cooking oil, salt, and pepper. Rinse chicken; pat dry with paper towels. Brush chicken with lime mixture.

Grill chicken on an uncovered grill directly over medium coals for 10 to 12 minutes or till chicken is tender and no longer pink, turning and brushing with lime mixture once. (*Or*, place chicken on the unheated rack of a broiler pan. Broil 5 to 6 inches from the heat for 12 to 15 minutes, turning and brushing with lime mixture once.) Serve with Pineapple Salsa. Makes 6 servings.

Pineapple Salsa: Place 1 pound fresh-cut *pineapple chunks* (3 cups) in a food processor bowl or blender container. Process or blend till chopped, but not pureed. Pour into large bowl. Add 1 large *tomato*, seeded and chopped; ½ cup chopped *red onion*; ½ cup chopped *red or green sweet pepper;* one (4-ounce) can diced *green chili peppers,* drained; 2 tablespoons snipped *cilantro;* ½ teaspoon finely shredded *lime peel;* 2 tablespoons *lime juice;* and 1 clove *garlic,* minced. Stir until mixed. Cover and chill till serving time. Makes 3 cups.

Nutrition information per serving: 177 calories, 19 g protein, 14 g carbohydrate, 5 g fat (1 g saturated), 50 mg cholesterol, 226 mg sodium, 354 mg potassium.

CHICKEN FAJITAS WITH GUACAMOLE

You can make this chunky guacamole up to 4 hours before serving. Just keep it covered and refrigerated so it won't darken.

¼ cup olive oil *or* cooking oil
¼ cup snipped cilantro *or* parsley
1 teaspoon finely shredded lemon peel
2 tablespoons lemon juice
1 teaspoon chili powder
½ teaspoon ground cumin
½ teaspoon pepper
12 ounces skinless, boneless chicken
      breasts
8 8-inch flour tortillas
2 cups shredded lettuce
1 cup shredded cheddar cheese
      (4 ounces)
1 large tomato, chopped
½ cup sliced pitted ripe olives
   Guacamole

For marinade, in a shallow nonmetallic dish combine oil, cilantro or parsley, lemon peel, lemon juice, chili powder, cumin, and pepper. Rinse chicken; pat dry with paper towels. Add chicken to marinade, turning to coat. Cover and chill about 1 hour.

Drain chicken, reserving marinade. Grill chicken on an uncovered grill directly over medium coals for 5 minutes. Turn chicken and brush with marinade; grill for 7 to 10 minutes more or till chicken is tender and no longer pink. (*Or,* place chicken on the unheated rack of a broiler pan. Broil 5 to 6 inches from the heat for 10 to 12 minutes, turning and brushing with marinade once.) Wrap flour tortillas in foil and heat on grill or in oven during the last 5 minutes of cooking chicken.

To serve, cut chicken into bite-sized strips. On each tortilla, arrange chicken strips, shredded lettuce, shredded cheese, chopped tomato, and sliced olives. Roll up tortillas, tucking in sides. Serve with Guacamole. Makes 4 servings.

Guacamole: Seed and peel 1 ripe *avocado.* In a mixing bowl coarsely mash avocado. Add 1 medium *tomato,* seeded, chopped, and drained; 2 tablespoons finely chopped *onion;* 1 tablespoon *lemon juice;* and ¼ teaspoon *salt.* Cover the surface of the guacamole with plastic wrap and chill up to 4 hours.

Nutrition information per serving: 576 calories, 30 g protein, 45 g carbohydrate, 32 g fat (10 g saturated), 74 mg cholesterol, 745 mg sodium, 736 mg potassium.

BARBECUED CHICKEN THIGHS

Thread chunks of red sweet pepper, corn on the cob, and zucchini on skewers for a quick partner to grill with the chicken thighs.

3   **tablespoons brown sugar**
2   **tablespoons finely chopped onion**
2   **tablespoons vinegar**
2   **tablespoons prepared mustard**
¼   **teaspoon celery seed**
⅛   **teaspoon garlic powder**
8   **chicken thighs (about 2½ pounds total)**
½   **teaspoon paprika**
¼   **teaspoon ground turmeric**
¼   **teaspoon salt**

For sauce, in a small saucepan combine brown sugar, onion, vinegar, mustard, celery seed, and garlic powder. Bring to boiling, stirring till the sugar dissolves. Remove from heat; set aside.

Skin chicken, if desired. Rinse chicken; pat dry with paper towels. In a small mixing bowl combine paprika, turmeric, and salt; rub over the chicken.

Grill chicken on an uncovered grill directly over medium coals for 20 minutes. Turn chicken; grill for 15 to 20 minutes more or till chicken is tender and no longer pink. (*Or,* place chicken on the unheated rack of a broiler pan. Broil 5 to 6 inches from the heat for 28 to 32 minutes, turning once.) Brush with sauce during the last 5 minutes of grilling or broiling. Makes 4 servings.

Nutrition information per serving: 375 calories, 37 g protein, 11 g carbohydrate, 19 g fat (5 g saturated), 129 mg cholesterol, 366 mg sodium, 388 mg potassium.

GRILLED CHICKEN WITH PEACH SALSA

This brightly colored peach salsa adds a flavor burst and a southwestern feel to the wine-marinated chicken.

4 chicken legs (thigh-drumstick piece)
   (about 2½ pounds total)
   Wine Marinade
2 medium peaches *or* nectarines *or*
   1⅓ cups frozen unsweetened peach
   slices, thawed
½ cup chopped red *or* green sweet
   pepper
½ ripe avocado, seeded, peeled, and
   finely chopped
2 green onions, finely chopped
½ teaspoon finely shredded lime peel
2 tablespoons lime juice
1 tablespoon snipped cilantro

Rinse chicken; pat dry with paper towels. Add chicken to Wine Marinade, turning to coat. Cover and chill about 1 hour.

Meanwhile, for salsa, peel and pit the fresh peaches or pit the nectarines. Finely chop peaches or nectarines. In a bowl combine peaches or nectarines, chopped red or green sweet pepper, avocado, green onions, lime peel, lime juice, and cilantro. Cover and chill till serving time.

Drain chicken, reserving marinade. Grill chicken, skin side down, on an uncovered grill directly over medium coals for 20 minutes. Turn chicken; grill for 15 to 20 minutes more or till chicken is tender and no longer pink. (*Or,* place chicken on the unheated rack of a broiler pan. Broil 5 to 6 inches from the heat for 28 to 32 minutes, turning once.) Brush with marinade up to last 5 minutes of grilling or broiling. Serve chicken with salsa. Makes 6 servings.

Wine Marinade: In a shallow nonmetallic dish combine ½ cup *dry white wine;* 1½ teaspoons finely shredded *orange peel;* ⅓ cup *orange juice;* 2 tablespoons *olive oil or cooking oil;* 1½ teaspoons snipped fresh *rosemary* or ½ teaspoon dried rosemary, crushed; and 1 *bay leaf.*

Nutrition information per serving: 311 calories, 25 g protein, 5 g carbohydrate, 20 g fat (4 g saturated), 86 mg cholesterol, 85 mg sodium, 531 mg potassium.

TEQUILA AND LIME CHICKEN

Flavors of a margarita enhance this simply delightful grilled chicken served with bottled salsa freshened with tomato, green onion, and cilantro.

- 2 teaspoons finely shredded lime peel
- ¼ cup lime juice
- ¼ cup tequila
- 1 tablespoon cooking oil
- 1 tablespoon orange liqueur *or*
  - 1 teaspoon finely shredded orange peel
- 2 cloves garlic, minced
- ¼ teaspoon salt
- ¼ teaspoon pepper
- 6 medium skinless, boneless chicken breast halves (about 1¼ pounds total)
- 1 cup hot chunky salsa
- 1 medium tomato, chopped
- 2 green onions, finely chopped
- 1 tablespoon snipped cilantro
- 2 tablespoons honey

In a shallow nonmetallic dish combine lime peel, lime juice, tequila, cooking oil, orange liqueur or orange peel, garlic, salt, and pepper. Rinse chicken; pat dry with paper towels. Add chicken to marinade, turning to coat. Cover and chill about 1 hour.

Meanwhile, for tomato salsa, in a small bowl combine chunky salsa, chopped tomato, green onions, and snipped cilantro; set aside.

Drain chicken, reserving marinade. Stir honey into marinade. Grill chicken on an uncovered grill directly over medium coals for 5 minutes. Turn chicken and brush with marinade; grill for 7 to 10 minutes more or till chicken is tender and no longer pink. (*Or,* place chicken on the unheated rack of a broiler pan. Broil 5 to 6 inches from the heat for 10 to 12 minutes, turning and brushing with marinade once.) Serve with tomato salsa. Makes 6 servings.

Nutrition information per serving: 201 calories, 19 g protein, 14 g carbohydrate, 6 g fat (1 g saturated), 50 mg cholesterol, 285 mg sodium, 364 mg potassium.

HERBED CHICKEN WITH SPINACH STUFFING

Serve wedges of roasted white or sweet potatoes on the side.

1 **5- to 6-pound whole roasting chicken**
1 **tablespoon olive oil** *or* **cooking oil**
1 **teaspoon dried basil, crushed**
1 **teaspoon dried oregano, crushed**
1 **teaspoon dried parsley flakes**
¼ **teaspoon garlic salt**
2 **10-ounce packages frozen chopped spinach, thawed and well drained**
1 **cup finely chopped red** *or* **green sweet pepper**
4 **ounces prosciutto** *or* **fully cooked boneless ham, chopped**
¾ **cup soft bread crumbs (1 slice)**
½ **cup sliced green onion**
⅓ **cup pine nuts** *or* **slivered almonds**
¼ **cup margarine** *or* **butter, melted**
¼ **teaspoon pepper**

Rinse chicken; pat dry with paper towels. Brush with oil. In a small bowl combine basil, oregano, parsley, and garlic salt; sprinkle on the outside of the bird, then rub in. Cover and chill for up to 24 hours.

For stuffing, in a large mixing bowl combine the spinach, red or green sweet pepper, prosciutto or ham, bread crumbs, green onion, pine nuts or almonds, melted margarine or butter, and pepper. Cover and chill for up to 24 hours, if desired.

Slip your fingers between the skin and breast meat of the bird, forming a pocket. Spoon some of stuffing into pocket. Spoon some of the stuffing loosely into the neck cavity. Pull neck skin to back; fasten with a small skewer. Lightly spoon the remaining stuffing into the body cavity. Tuck drumsticks under the band of skin that crosses the tail. If there is no band, tie drumsticks to the tail. Twist the wing tips under the chicken.

Place stuffed chicken, breast side up, on a rack in a shallow roasting pan. Insert a meat thermometer into the center of one of the thigh muscles. The bulb should not touch the bone. Roast, uncovered, in a 325° oven for 1¾ to 2½ hours or till meat thermometer registers 180° to 185°. At this time, chicken is no longer pink and the drumsticks move easily in their sockets. When the bird is two-thirds done, cut the band of skin or string between the drumsticks so the thighs will cook evenly.

Remove chicken from oven and cover it with foil. Let stand 10 to 20 minutes before carving. Makes 10 servings.

Nutrition information per serving: 514 calories, 38 g protein, 7 g carbohydrate, 38 g fat (8 g saturated), 93 mg cholesterol, 586 mg sodium, 516 mg potassium.

ROASTED CHICKEN WITH CHERRY SAUCE

You can skip the brandy in the cherry sauce if you wish--just add a little more apple juice.

- 1 **5- to 6-pound whole roasting chicken**
- 1 **tablespoon olive oil *or* cooking oil**
- ½ **teaspoon garlic powder**
- ½ **teaspoon dried tarragon, crushed**
- ¼ **teaspoon salt**
- ¼ **teaspoon pepper**
- ½ **medium lemon, sliced**
- 1 **sprig parsley**
- 3 **tablespoons brown sugar**
- 4 **teaspoons cornstarch**
- 2 **cups frozen tart red cherries**
- ¾ **cup apple juice**
- 1 **tablespoon lemon juice**
- 2 **tablespoons brandy**

Rinse chicken. Pat dry with paper towels. Brush with olive oil or cooking oil. In a small bowl combine garlic powder, tarragon, salt, and pepper; sprinkle on the outside of the bird, then rub in. Place lemon slices and parsley in body cavity. Tuck the drumsticks under the band of skin that crosses the tail. If there is no band, tie drumsticks to the tail. Twist the wing tips under the bird.

Place chicken, breast side up, on a rack in a shallow roasting pan. Insert a meat thermometer into the center of one of the thigh muscles. The bulb should not touch the bone. Roast, uncovered, in a 325° oven for 1¾ to 2½ hours or till meat thermometer registers 180° to 185°. At this time, chicken is no longer pink and the drumsticks move easily in their sockets. When the bird is two-thirds done, cut the band of skin or string between the drumsticks so the thighs will cook evenly Remove chicken from oven and cover it with foil. Let stand 10 to 20 minutes before carving.

Meanwhile, for sauce, in a medium saucepan stir together the brown sugar and cornstarch. Stir in the cherries, apple juice, and lemon juice. Cook and stir till thickened and bubbly. Cook and stir for 2 minutes more. Stir in brandy. Heat through. Serve sauce with chicken. Makes 10 servings.

Nutrition information per serving: 304 calories, 32 g protein, 11 g carbohydrate, 14 g fat (4 g saturated), 93 mg cholesterol, 212 mg sodium, 363 mg potassium.

MINNESOTA WILD RICE-STUFFED CHICKEN

Team up this bird with a chicory and red onion salad dressed with a blue cheese vinaigrette.

1   **6-ounce package long grain and wild
    rice mix**
2   **medium cooking apples (such as
    Granny Smith *or* Jonathan), cored
    and chopped**
8   **ounces sliced fresh mushrooms
    (3 cups)**
1   **cup shredded carrot**
½   **cup thinly sliced green onion**
½   **teaspoon pepper**
1   **5-to 6-pound whole roasting chicken**
2   **to 3 tablespoons apple jelly, melted**
    Apple wedges (optional)

For stuffing, cook rice according to package directions, *except* add apples, mushrooms, carrot, onion, and pepper to rice before cooking.

Meanwhile, rinse chicken; pat dry with paper towels. Spoon some of the stuffing loosely into the neck cavity. Pull the neck skin to the back and fasten with a small skewer. Lightly spoon the remaining stuffing into body cavity. Tuck drumsticks under the band of skin that crosses the tail. If there is no band, tie drumsticks to tail. Twist the wing tips under the bird.

Place stuffed chicken, breast side up, on a rack in a shallow roasting pan. Insert meat thermometer into the center of one of the thigh muscles. The bulb should not touch the bone. Roast, uncovered, in a 325° oven for 1¾ to 2½ hours or till meat thermometer registers 180° to 185°. At this time, chicken is no longer pink and the drumsticks move easily in their sockets. When the bird is two-thirds done, cut the band of skin or string between the drumsticks so the thighs will cook evenly. Brush chicken with melted jelly once or twice during the last 10 minutes of roasting.

Remove chicken from oven and cover it with foil. Let stand for 10 to 20 minutes before carving. Transfer the chicken to a serving platter. Spoon the stuffing around the chicken. Garnish with apple wedges, if desired. Makes 10 servings.

Nutrition information per serving: 332 calories, 34 g protein, 19 g carbohydrate, 13 g fat (4 g saturated), 93 mg cholesterol, 365 mg sodium, 408 mg potassium.

ROASTED PESTO CHICKEN
Steamed baby carrots with tops make an easy, but special vegetable accompaniment.

1   **5- to 6-pound whole roasting chicken**
    Basil-Walnut Pesto
1   **clove garlic, minced**
2   **tablespoons margarine *or* butter**
2   **tablespoons all-purpose flour**
1   **cup chicken broth**
2   **tablespoons dry white wine**
    Basil leaves (optional)

Rinse chicken; pat dry with paper towels. Slip your fingers between the skin and breast meat of the bird and between the skin and leg meat, forming pockets. Spoon some of the Basil-Walnut Pesto into pockets. Spoon some of the pesto loosely into the neck cavity. Pull neck skin to back; fasten with a small skewer. Lightly spoon some of the pesto into the body cavity. Rub remaining pesto over outside of chicken. Tuck drumsticks under the band of skin that crosses the tail. If there is no band, tie drumsticks to the tail. Twist the wing tips under the chicken.

Place chicken, breast side up, on rack in shallow roasting pan. Insert a meat thermometer into the center of one of the thigh muscles. The bulb should not touch bone. Roast, uncovered, in a 325° oven for 1¾ to 2½ hours or till meat thermometer registers 180° to 185°. At this time, chicken is no longer pink and the drumsticks move easily in their sockets. When the bird is two-thirds done, cut the band of skin or string between the drumsticks so the thighs cook evenly. Transfer chicken to a platter. Let stand 10 to 20 minutes before carving.

Meanwhile, for sauce, in a small saucepan cook garlic in margarine or butter. Stir in flour. Add broth and white wine. Cook and stir till thickened and bubbly. Cook and stir for 1 minute more. Serve sauce with sliced chicken. Garnish with basil, if desired. Makes 10 servings.

Basil-Walnut Pesto: In a food processor bowl or blender container combine 1 cup lightly packed fresh *basil,* ½ cup chopped *walnuts;* and 2 cloves *garlic,* minced. Process or blend till mixed. Leave motor running and add ¼ cup *olive oil* in a slow steady stream. Turn off. Add ½ cup grated *Parmesan cheese* and coarsely ground *pepper* to taste. Process or blend until smooth. Makes about ¾ cup pesto.

Nutrition information per serving: 391 calories, 35 g protein, 3 g carbohydrate, 26 g fat (6 g saturated), 97 mg cholesterol, 252 mg sodium, 366 mg potassium.

FRUIT-STUFFED ROASTED CHICKEN

While the bird roasts to perfection, tuck some rice pudding in the oven to bake alongside.

1   **5- to 6-pound whole roasting chicken**
    Salt
    Pepper
¼   **cup margarine *or* butter, melted**
¼   **cup dry sherry**
4½ **teaspoons snipped fresh thyme *or***
       1½ teaspoons dried thyme, crushed
2   **teaspoons finely shredded orange peel**
2   **medium apples, cored and chopped**
       (2 cups)
1   **medium onion, chopped (½ cup)**
½   **cup chopped celery**
2   **cups cubed French bread (¾-inch**
       cubes)
10 **pitted prunes *or* dried apricot halves,**
       cut up
1   **cup seedless green grapes, halved**
2   **tablespoons orange juice**

Rinse chicken; pat dry with paper towels. Season body cavity with salt and pepper. In a small bowl combine *2 tablespoons* of the melted margarine, *2 tablespoons* of the dry sherry, *1 tablespoon* of the fresh thyme or *1 teaspoon* of the dried thyme, and *1 teaspoon* of the orange peel; mix well. Brush bird with sherry mixture.

For stuffing, in a medium skillet cook apples, onion, and celery in remaining melted margarine about 5 minutes or till tender. In a large mixing bowl combine apple mixture with cubed French bread, prunes or apricots, grapes, orange juice, remaining dry sherry, remaining fresh or dried thyme, and remaining orange peel. Mix well. (Stuffing will become more moist while cooking.) Spoon some of the stuffing loosely into the neck cavity. Pull neck skin to back; fasten with a small skewer. Lightly spoon the remaining stuffing into the body cavity. Tuck drumsticks under the band of skin that crosses the tail. If there is no band, tie drumsticks to the tail. Twist the wing tips under the chicken.

Place stuffed chicken, breast side up, on a rack in a shallow roasting pan. Insert a meat thermometer into the center of one of the thigh muscles. The bulb should not touch the bone. Roast, uncovered, in a 325° oven for 1¾ to 2½ hours or till meat thermometer registers 180° to 185°. At this time, chicken is no longer pink and the drumsticks move easily in their sockets. When the bird is two-thirds done, cut the band of skin or string between the drumsticks so the thighs will cook evenly.

Remove bird from oven and cover it with foil. Let bird stand 10 to 20 minutes before carving. Makes 10 servings.

Nutrition information per serving: 393 calories, 33 g protein, 22 g carbohydrate, 18 g fat (5 g saturated), 93 mg cholesterol, 250 mg sodium, 475 mg potassium.

ROAST CHICKEN SOUTHWESTERN-STYLE

Squares of freshly baked corn bread add just the right touch to this easy-to-make roasted chicken.

1 **5- to 6-pound whole roasting chicken**
1 **tablespoon olive oil *or* cooking oil**
1 **teaspoon dried oregano, crushed**
½ **teaspoon ground cumin**
1 **lime, cut into 6 wedges**
2 **cilantro sprigs**
1 **15-ounce can black beans, rinsed and drained**
1 **small tomato, chopped**
1 **small cucumber, seeded and chopped**
¼ **cup chopped green onion**
2 **tablespoons snipped cilantro *or* parsley**
1 **teaspoon finely shredded lime peel**
2 **tablespoons lime juice**
1 **tablespoon olive oil *or* cooking oil**
1 **clove garlic, minced**
¼ **teaspoon salt**
   Cilantro sprigs (optional)
   Lime wedges (optional)

Rinse chicken; pat dry with paper towels. Brush with 1 tablespoon oil. In a small bowl combine oregano and cumin; sprinkle over the outside of the bird, then rub into skin. Place 6 lime wedges and 2 cilantro sprigs in body cavity. Tuck the drumsticks under the band of skin that crosses the tail. If there is no band, tie drumsticks to the tail. Twist the wing tips under the chicken.

Place chicken, breast side up, on a rack in a shallow pan. Insert a meat thermometer into the center of one of the thigh muscles. The bulb should not touch the bone. Roast, uncovered, in a 325° oven for 1¾ to 2½ hours or till meat thermometer registers 180° to 185°. At this time, chicken is no longer pink and the drumsticks move easily in their sockets. When the bird is two-thirds done, cut the band of skin or string between the drumsticks so the thighs cook more evenly.

Meanwhile, for black bean salsa, in a bowl combine black beans, tomato, cucumber, green onion, cilantro or parsley, lime peel, lime juice, 1 tablespoon oil, garlic, and salt. Mix well. Cover and chill until serving time.

Remove chicken from oven and cover it with foil. Let chicken stand for 10 to 20 minutes before carving. Serve black bean salsa with chicken. Garnish with additional cilantro and lime wedges, if desired. Makes 10 servings.

Nutrition information per serving: 310 calories, 35 g protein, 9 g carbohydrate, 16 g fat (4 g saturated), 93 mg cholesterol, 214 mg sodium, 448 mg potassium.

CHICKEN SALAD WITH RASPBERRY VINAIGRETTE

If you like, arrange all the ingredients on a large glass salad plate and pass the dressing in a small cruet.

2 cups torn leaf lettuce
2 cups torn radicchio
2 cups torn arugula
1 medium Belgian endive, cut up
4 skinless, boneless large chicken breast halves (about 1 pound total)
1 tablespoon Dijon-style mustard
1 tablespoon honey
¼ teaspoon salt
⅛ teaspoon pepper
2 medium oranges, peeled and sliced
1 avocado, halved, seeded, peeled, and sliced lengthwise
1 pink grapefruit, peeled and sectioned
2 green onions, thinly bias sliced
Raspberry Vinaigrette
Raspberries (optional)

In a bowl combine leaf lettuce, radicchio, arugula, and Belgian endive. Toss lightly to mix. Cover and chill up to 2 hours.

Rinse chicken; pat dry with paper towels. Combine Dijon-style mustard, honey, salt, and pepper; set aside. Grill chicken on an uncovered grill directly over medium coals about 15 minutes or till tender and no longer pink, turning once and brushing with mustard mixture during the last 2 minutes of grilling. Cool chicken slightly; slice into ¼-inch strips.

On each individual salad plate, arrange greens. Top with chicken strips, oranges, avocado slices, and grapefruit sections. Sprinkle green onions over all. Drizzle each salad with some of the Raspberry Vinaigrette. Garnish with raspberries, if desired. Makes 4 servings.

Raspberry Vinaigrette: In a blender container combine one 10-ounce package frozen *red raspberries,* thawed; 2 tablespoons *olive oil or salad oil;* 2 tablespoons *lemon juice;* and 1 clove *garlic,* minced. Cover and blend till smooth. Use a sieve to strain dressing; discard seeds. Cover and chill dressing till serving time. Reserve any remaining vinaigrette for another use. Makes 1½ cups.

Nutrition information per serving: 331 calories, 25 g protein, 26 g carbohydrate, 15 g fat (1 g saturated), 59 mg cholesterol, 295 mg sodium, 916 mg potassium.

SOUTHWESTERN CHICKEN AND BLACK BEAN SALAD

A refreshing main-dish salad that combines the flavors of cilantro, lime juice, and black beans.

12 ounces skinless, boneless chicken
     thighs *or* breasts
½ teaspoon chili powder
½ teaspoon ground cumin
¼ teaspoon salt
⅛ teaspoon ground red pepper
1 tablespoon olive oil *or* cooking oil
3 cups torn romaine *or* mixed greens
1 15-ounce can black beans, rinsed and
     drained
2 large oranges, peeled and sectioned
2 slices red onion, halved and separated
     into rings
   Citrus Dressing

Rinse chicken; pat dry with paper towels. Cut chicken into thin, bite-sized strips. In a large skillet cook chili powder, cumin, salt, and red pepper in hot oil over medium-high heat for 30 seconds. Add chicken strips and cook for 2 to 3 minutes or till lightly browned and no longer pink.

In a salad bowl combine chicken, romaine or mixed greens, black beans, orange sections, and sliced red onion. Cover and chill salad up to 2 hours. To serve, pour the Citrus Dressing over the salad. Toss lightly to coat. Makes 4 servings.

Citrus Dressing: In a screw-top jar combine ¼ cup snipped *cilantro;* ¼ cup *olive or salad oil;* 2 tablespoons *lime juice;* 2 tablespoons *orange juice;* 1 clove *garlic,* minced; and ⅛ teaspoon *salt.* Cover and shake well. Chill till serving time. Shake well before using. Makes ½ cup.

Nutrition information per serving: 340 calories, 24 g protein, 22 g carbohydrate, 20 g fat (3 g saturated), 45 mg cholesterol, 515 mg sodium, 578 mg potassium.

CHICKEN NOODLE SALAD WITH PEANUT DRESSING

Although the flavors blend upon chilling, if you would prefer, serve this salad right after tossing.

6 ounces linguine *or* very thin spaghetti
2 cups cooked chicken cut into strips (10 ounces)
1 medium cucumber, halved lengthwise, seeded and sliced
1 cup fresh pea pods, strings removed and bias sliced in ½-inch pieces
4 green onions, cut into ½-inch pieces
1 medium tomato, chopped
Soy Peanut Dressing
2 cups shredded napa cabbage
2 cups shredded spinach
¼ cup chopped peanuts

Cook pasta according to package directions for al dente. Drain; rinse under cold water.

In a bowl combine linguine, chicken strips, cucumber, pea pods, green onions, and tomato. Pour the Soy Peanut Dressing over noodle mixture. Toss gently to mix. Cover and chill chicken mixture for 4 to 24 hours, stirring mixture 2 to 3 times.

To serve, line 4 dinner or salad plates with the shredded napa cabbage and spinach. Top with chicken mixture. Sprinkle with peanuts. Makes 4 servings.

Soy Peanut Dressing: In a blender container combine ¾ cup *water;* ¼ cup *peanut butter;* ¼ cup *soy sauce;* 2 tablespoons *red wine vinegar;* 2 tablespoons *olive oil or salad oil;* 1 tablespoon *sugar;* 1 tablespoon *toasted sesame oil;* 1 tablespoon *lemon juice;* 1 teaspoon grated *ginger-root;* 1 clove *garlic,* minced; and 1 teaspoon *chili paste or ½ teaspoon crushed red pepper.* Cover and blend till smooth. Makes about 2 cups.

Nutrition information per serving: 620 calories, 39 g protein, 53 g carbohydrate, 30 g fat (5 g saturated), 68 mg cholesterol, 1,139 mg sodium, 954 mg potassium.

THAI CHICKEN SALAD

Look for the fish sauce and lemongrass in an Oriental grocery store or the gourmet section of your supermarket.

1   pound skinless, boneless chicken breasts
2   tablespoons olive oil *or* salad oil
1   teaspoon chili powder
½   teaspoon garlic powder
¼   teaspoon white pepper
¼   teaspoon black pepper
4   cups torn romaine
1   cup torn radicchio
1   Belgian endive, cut up
1   medium tomato, chopped
2   tablespoons snipped fresh mint *or* Thai basil
    Lemon Dressing
    Mint leaves (optional)

Rinse chicken; pat dry with paper towels. Combine *1 tablespoon* of the olive oil or salad oil, the chili powder, garlic powder, white pepper, and black pepper. Coat chicken with mixture. In a large skillet cook chicken in remaining hot oil over medium heat for 8 to 10 minutes or till tender and no longer pink, turning once. Cool slightly; cut chicken into thin strips.

In a salad bowl combine chicken strips, romaine, radicchio, Belgian endive, tomato, and snipped mint or Thai basil. Cover and chill salad up to 2 hours.

To serve, drizzle the Lemon Dressing over the salad. Toss lightly to coat. Garnish with mint leaves, if desired. Makes 4 servings.

Lemon Dressing: In a screw-top jar combine ¼ cup *olive oil or salad oil;* 3 tablespoons *lemon juice;* 1 tablespoon *fish sauce;* 1 tablespoon *honey;* 1 tablespoon finely chopped fresh *lemongrass* or ½ teaspoon finely shredded lemon peel; 1 clove *garlic,* minced; and ½ teaspoon *crushed red pepper.* Cover and shake well. Chill dressing till serving time. Shake well before using.

Nutrition information per serving: 352 calories, 24 g protein, 11 g carbohydrate, 24 g fat (4 g saturated), 59 mg cholesterol, 298 mg sodium, 516 mg potassium.

CAESAR CHICKEN SALAD

When you add chicken to this traditional salad, it turns into a simple main dish, especially when served with crusty bread.

¼ **cup salad oil**
¼ **cup egg product**
2 **tablespoons red wine vinegar**
1 **tablespoon lemon juice**
1 **clove garlic, minced**
1 **teaspoon anchovy paste** *or*
   2 anchovy fillets
½ **teaspoon Worcestershire sauce**
6 **cups torn romaine**
2 **cups cubed cooked chicken**
   (10 ounces)
4 **green onions, bias sliced**
¼ **cup finely shredded Parmesan cheese**
   Garlic Croutons
   Coarsely ground pepper

For dressing, in a blender container combine oil, egg product, vinegar, lemon juice, garlic, anchovy paste, and Worcestershire sauce. Cover and blend until smooth.

In a large salad bowl combine romaine, chicken, green onions, Parmesan cheese, and Garlic Croutons. Pour the dressing over the salad. Toss gently and serve immediately. Pass coarsely ground pepper. Makes 6 servings.

Garlic Croutons: In a medium skillet over medium heat cook 1 clove *garlic,* minced, in 2 tablespoons *olive oil or salad oil* just till golden. Add 2 cups cubed *French bread,* stirring to coat evenly. Transfer bread cubes to a shallow baking pan. Bake in a 300° oven for 10 minutes. Stir. Bake about 5 minutes more or till the cubes are dry and crisp. Makes about 2 cups.

Nutrition information per serving: 316 calories, 21 g protein, 12 g carbohydrate, 21 g fat (4 g saturated), 50 mg cholesterol, 296 mg sodium, 356 mg potassium.

WARM CHICKEN SPINACH SALAD

Another main-dish salad perfect for summertime entertaining.

6 **cups torn spinach**
2 **cups torn leaf lettuce**
1 **medium red onion, thinly sliced**
2 **red *or* green sweet peppers, cut into bite-sized strips**
12 **ounces skinless, boneless chicken breasts**
½ **teaspoon dried rosemary, crushed**
½ **teaspoon lemon-pepper seasoning**
1 **clove garlic, minced**
1 **tablespoon cooking oil**
2 **tablespoons balsamic vinegar**
2 **tablespoons water**
Fresh rosemary sprigs (optional)

In a large salad bowl, combine spinach, leaf lettuce, sliced red onion, and pepper strips. Cover and chill salad up to 2 hours.

Rinse chicken; pat dry with paper towels. Cut chicken into bite-sized strips. Toss chicken with rosemary and lemon-pepper seasoning. In a 10-inch skillet stir-fry chicken strips and garlic in hot oil over medium-high heat for 2 to 3 minutes or till chicken is tender and no longer pink. Remove chicken from skillet. Add to salad mixture.

For dressing, add vinegar and water to skillet, stirring to scrape up any browned bits. Pour dressing over salad. Toss gently to mix. Transfer to individual salad plates. Garnish with fresh rosemary, if desired. Makes 4 servings.

Nutrition information per serving: 172 calories, 20 g protein, 10 g carbohydrate, 6 g fat (1 g saturated), 45 mg cholesterol, 248 mg sodium, 781 mg potassium.

ORIENTAL CHICKEN SALAD

Canned mandarin orange segments make a quick substitute for the fresh orange.

3 ounces dry Chinese egg noodles *or* fine egg noodles
1 pound skinless, boneless chicken breasts *or* thighs
1 green onion, chopped
2 sprigs parsley
½ lemon, sliced
3 cups torn Boston lettuce
1 cup red *or* green sweet pepper cut into thin strips
1 orange, peeled and sectioned
1 8-ounce can bamboo shoots, drained
   Soy Ginger Dressing
   Lime slices (optional)

Cook noodles according to package directions. Drain; set aside. (You should have 2 cups.) Rinse chicken; pat dry with paper towels.

In a 10-inch skillet place green onion, parsley sprigs, and lemon slices. Add enough water to fill to a depth of 1 inch. Bring to boiling; add chicken. Cover and simmer about 15 minutes or till chicken is tender and no longer pink. Drain; discard liquid and seasoning. Cool chicken; cut into bite-sized strips.

In a salad bowl combine chicken, Boston lettuce, red or green sweet pepper, orange segments, bamboo shoots, and cooked Chinese noodles. Cover and chill salad for up to 2 hours. To serve, pour Soy Ginger Dressing over salad. Toss gently to mix. Garnish with lime slices, if desired. Makes 6 servings.

Soy Ginger Dressing: In a screw-top jar combine 3 tablespoons *olive oil or salad oil;* 2 tablespoons *lime juice;* 2 tablespoons *soy sauce;* 1 teaspoon grated *gingerroot;* and 1 clove *garlic,* minced. Cover and shake well. Chill dressing till serving time. Shake dressing well before using. Makes about ½ cup.

Nutrition information per serving: 213 calories, 18 g protein, 14 g carbohydrate, 10 g fat (2 g saturated), 52 mg cholesterol, 386 mg sodium, 288 mg potassium.

ORANGE CHICKEN SALAD

Fresh fruit flavors and the subtle orange dressing characterize this pretty-as-a-picture salad.

1 medium pineapple, peeled, cored, and
　　cut into 1-inch chunks (3 cups)
2 cups cubed cooked chicken
　　(10 ounces)
2 oranges, peeled, halved, and sliced
1 cup seedless green grapes, halved
1 cup sliced strawberries
1 kiwi fruit, peeled and sliced
　　Lettuce leaves (optional)
　　Orange Yogurt Dressing
½ cup toasted slivered almonds

In a large bowl combine pineapple chunks, chicken, orange slices, grapes, strawberries, and kiwi fruit. Toss gently to mix.

Line six salad plates with lettuce, if desired. Spoon mixture onto salad plates. Drizzle with Orange Yogurt Dressing. Sprinkle with almonds. Makes 6 servings.

Orange Yogurt Dressing: In small mixing bowl combine ⅓ cup *non-fat cream cheese product,* ½ cup *low-fat vanilla yogurt,* 1 teaspoon finely shredded *orange peel,* 2 tablespoons *orange juice,* and ⅛ teaspoon ground *nutmeg.* Stir until smooth. Cover and chill till serving time. Makes about ¾ cup.

Nutrition information per serving: 275 calories, 22 g protein, 28 g carbohydrate, 10 g fat (2 g saturated), 48 mg cholesterol, 142 mg sodium, 517 mg potassium.

TEX-MEX CHICKEN TOSTADAS

Ground chicken makes quick work of this Tex-Mex open-face sandwich.

4 **8-inch flour tortillas**
1 **pound ground raw chicken**
1 **teaspoon chili powder**
1 **8-ounce bottle medium** *or* **hot salsa**
1 **15-ounce can black beans** *or* **pinto beans**
2 **tablespoons diced pimiento**
1 **cup chopped lettuce**
¼ **cup thinly sliced radishes**
¼ **cup shredded cheddar cheese (1 ounce)**
1 **2¼-ounce can sliced pitted ripe olives**
   Dairy sour cream (optional)
2 **tablespoons thinly sliced green onion**
   Avocado slices (optional)

For tostada shells, place tortillas in a single layer directly on the middle oven rack. Bake in a 350° oven about 6 minutes, turning halfway through baking time, or till golden and crisp. (If tortillas bubble during baking, puncture the bubble with a fork.) Set aside and cover to keep warm.

Meanwhile, in a 10-inch skillet cook and stir chicken and chili powder over medium heat for 5 to 7 minutes or till chicken is no longer pink. Stir in salsa. Set aside; keep warm.

Drain beans, reserving liquid. In a small saucepan stir beans over low heat till heated through. With a potato masher or fork, mash beans adding enough reserved bean liquid to make spreadable consistency. Heat through.

To assemble, place a warm tortilla on each dinner plate. Spread with a thin layer of beans. Top beans with some of the chicken mixture, pimiento, lettuce, radishes, cheese, olives, sour cream (if desired), and green onion. Garnish with avocado, if desired. Makes 4 servings.

Nutrition information per serving: 365 calories, 29 g protein, 38 g carbohydrate, 15 g fat (4 g saturated), 62 mg cholesterol, 809 mg sodium, 640 mg potassium.

GRILLED HONEY-SOY CHICKEN SANDWICHES

Fresh fruit is all you need to complete the meal.

⅓ cup orange juice
2 tablespoons reduced-sodium soy sauce
2 tablespoons honey
2 teaspoons lemon-pepper seasoning
1 teaspoon ground ginger
¼ teaspoon garlic powder
4 medium skinless, boneless chicken breast halves (about 12 ounces total)
4 whole wheat hamburger buns
 Lettuce leaves
1 plum tomato, sliced

In a shallow, nonmetallic dish combine orange juice, soy sauce, honey, lemon-pepper seasoning, ginger, and garlic powder. Set aside.

Rinse chicken; pat dry with paper towels. Place each breast half between 2 pieces of plastic wrap. Working from center to the edges, pound lightly with the flat side of a meat mallet to an even thickness. Remove plastic wrap. Place chicken pieces in marinade. Cover and chill for 4 to 6 hours or overnight.

Remove chicken from marinade, reserving marinade. To grill, place chicken on an uncovered grill directly over medium coals. Grill about 12 minutes or till tender and no longer pink, turning and brushing chicken with marinade once. (*Or,* place chicken on the unheated rack of a broiler pan. Broil 4 to 5 inches from heat about 7 minutes, turning and brushing chicken with marinade once.)

Split buns and place on grill rack or broiler pan for 1 to 2 minutes to toast. Serve chicken breasts on toasted buns. Top each with lettuce and tomato slices. Makes 4 servings.

Nutrition information per serving: 263 calories, 21 g protein, 33 g carbohydrate, 5 g fat (1 g saturated), 45 mg cholesterol, 1,106 mg sodium, 309 mg potassium.

CHICKEN PATTIES ON CROISSANTS

These oval burgers are great in the round, too, served on hamburger buns.

1   **beaten egg**
½   **cup finely chopped celery**
½   **cup finely chopped green sweet
      pepper**
⅓   **cup fine dry seasoned bread crumbs**
2   **tablespoons finely chopped onion**
1   **tablespoon snipped parsley**
1   **teaspoon Worcestershire sauce**
¼   **teaspoon salt**
1   **pound ground raw chicken**
2   **tablespoons cooking oil**
4   **croissants, split lengthwise
      Creamy Tarragon Sauce**
4   **lettuce leaves**
1   **large tomato, sliced**

In medium mixing bowl combine egg, celery, green sweet pepper, bread crumbs, onion, parsley, Worcestershire sauce, and salt. Add chicken; mix lightly but well. Shape into four 4-inch oval patties.

In large skillet cook chicken patties in hot oil over medium heat for 10 to 12 minutes or till no longer pink, turning once. Spread each cut side of croissants with some of the Creamy Tarragon Sauce. Arrange a lettuce leaf and a chicken patty on bottom half of each croissant. Top each with a tomato slice and croissant top. Serve with any remaining Creamy Tarragon Sauce. Makes 4 sandwiches.

Creamy Tarragon Sauce: In small bowl combine ½ cup *mayonnaise or salad dressing;* 1 tablespoon finely chopped *green onion;* 1 teaspoon snipped *parsley;* ⅛ teaspoon dried *tarragon,* crushed; and a dash *pepper.* Stir to mix. Cover and chill until serving time. Makes ½ cup.

Nutrition information per serving: 560 calories, 22 g protein, 23 g carbohydrate, 43 g fat (10 g saturated), 153 mg cholesterol, 610 mg sodium, 441 mg potassium.

HAWAIIAN CHICKEN BURGERS

Serve with pineapple spritzers--just pour pineapple juice over ice in glasses filling about one-third full and top with club soda.

1   beaten egg
¼   cup fine dry seasoned bread crumbs
3   tablespoons chopped water chestnuts
¾   teaspoon ground ginger
¼   teaspoon salt
¼   teaspoon pepper
1   pound ground raw chicken
¼   cup bottled sweet-and-sour sauce
4   canned pineapple rings
4   kaiser rolls *or* hamburger buns, split
    and toasted
    Shredded spinach

In a medium bowl combine egg, bread crumbs, water chestnuts, ginger, salt, and pepper. Add ground chicken and mix well. Shape into four ¾-inch-thick patties.

To grill, place patties on an uncovered grill directly over medium coals; cook for 15 to 18 minutes or till no longer pink, turning once and brushing with sweet-and-sour sauce during last 5 minutes of cooking. Meanwhile, place pineapple slices on grill rack. Cook for 5 minutes, turning as needed.

To serve burgers, sprinkle bottom half of each bun with some shredded spinach. Top with patties. Brush patties with sweet-and-sour sauce and top with pineapple slices. Makes 4 servings.

Nutrition information per serving: 331 calories, 23 g protein, 37 g carbohydrate, 9 g fat (2 g saturated), 108 mg cholesterol, 1,092 mg sodium, 376 mg potassium.

CHICKEN OLIVE CALZONES

Whether served warm with spaghetti sauce or at room temperature from a lunch bag, these sandwiches will be a family favorite.

1½ cups chopped cooked chicken
    (8 ounces)
½ cup shredded Monterey Jack cheese
¼ cup chopped celery
¼ cup chopped pitted ripe olives
½ teaspoon dried basil, crushed
¼ teaspoon dried oregano, crushed
⅛ teaspoon garlic powder
⅛ teaspoon pepper
⅓ cup soft-style cream cheese with
    chives and onion
1 10-ounce package refrigerated pizza
    dough
1 beaten egg
1 tablespoon water
    Grated Parmesan cheese (optional)
    Spaghetti sauce (optional)

For filling, in a medium bowl combine chicken, Monterey Jack cheese, celery, ripe olives, basil, oregano, garlic powder, and pepper. Stir in soft-style cream cheese. Set aside.

For calzones, unroll pizza dough. On lightly floured surface roll dough into a 15x10-inch rectangle. Cut into six 5-inch squares. Divide chicken-olive filling among the squares. Brush edges with water. Lift one corner and stretch dough over to the opposite corner. Seal edges of dough well with tines of a fork. Arrange calzones on a greased baking sheet. Prick tops with a fork. In a small bowl combine egg and 1 tablespoon water; brush over the calzones. Sprinkle with Parmesan cheese, if desired.

Bake in a 425° oven for 10 to 12 minutes or till golden brown. Let stand for 5 minutes before serving. Serve with heated spaghetti sauce, if desired. Makes 6 calzones.

Nutrition information per serving: 268 calories, 18 g protein, 19 g carbohydrate, 13 g fat (5 g saturated), 90 mg cholesterol, 320 mg sodium, 198 mg potassium.

CHICKEN IN A PITA

Other wrappers also work well for this filling--try warm flour tortillas or a more traditional soft roll.

12	ounces skinless, boneless chicken breasts
2	tablespoons olive oil *or* cooking oil
½	teaspoon dried oregano, crushed
¼	teaspoon garlic powder
¼	teaspoon salt
¼	teaspoon coarsely ground pepper
4	8-inch pita bread rounds
4	lettuce leaves
1	small tomato, chopped
½	cup alfalfa sprouts
	Cucumber Yogurt Sauce

Rinse chicken; pat dry with paper towels. Brush chicken with *1 tablespoon* of the oil. In a small bowl combine oregano, garlic powder, salt, and pepper; sprinkle on chicken breasts.

In large skillet cook chicken in remaining hot oil over medium heat about 10 minutes or till chicken is tender and no longer pink. Cool slightly; cut into thin strips.

On each pita place a lettuce leaf. Top with chicken strips, tomato, and alfalfa sprouts. Drizzle with Cucumber Yogurt Sauce. Fold pitas in half and wrap with a paper napkin to secure. Serve immediately. Makes 4 sandwiches.

Cucumber Yogurt Sauce: In a small bowl combine ½ cup *plain nonfat yogurt;* ¼ cup chopped, seeded *cucumber;* 1 tablespoon finely chopped *onion;* 1 tablespoon snipped *parsley;* ½ teaspoon *lemon juice;* and ⅛ teaspoon *garlic powder.* Stir to mix. Cover and chill until serving time. Makes 1 cup sauce.

Nutrition information per serving: 285 calories, 23 g protein, 26 g carbohydrate, 10 g fat (2 g saturated), 45 mg cholesterol, 423 mg sodium, 376 mg potassium.

Keep track of your daily nutrition needs by using the information we provide at the end of each recipe. We've analyzed the nutritional content of each recipe serving for you. When a recipe gives an ingredient substitution, we used the first choice in the analysis. If it makes a range of servings (such as 4 to 6), we used the smallest number. Ingredients listed as optional weren't included in the calculations.

METRIC COOKING HINTS

By making a few conversions, cooks in Australia, Canada, and the United Kingdom can use the recipes in Better Homes and Gardens® *Chicken* with confidence. The charts on this page provide a guide for converting measurements from the U.S. customary system, which is used throughout this book, to the imperial and metric systems. There also is a conversion table for oven temperatures to accommodate the differences in oven calibrations.

Volume and Weight: Americans traditionally use cup measures for liquid and solid ingredients. The chart (top right) shows the approximate imperial and metric equivalents. If you are accustomed to weighing solid ingredients, here are some helpful approximate equivalents.
■ 1 cup butter, caster sugar, or rice = 8 ounces = about 250 grams
■ 1 cup flour = 4 ounces = about 125 grams
■ 1 cup icing sugar = 5 ounces = about 150 grams
   Spoon measures are used for smaller amounts of ingredients. Although the size of the tablespoon varies slightly among countries, for practical purposes and for recipes in this book, a straight substitution is all that's necessary.
   Measurements made using cups or spoons should always be level, unless stated otherwise.

Product Differences: Most of the ingredients called for in the recipes in this book are available in English-speaking countries. However, some are known by different names. Here are some common American ingredients and their possible counterparts:
■ Sugar is granulated or caster sugar.
■ Powdered sugar is icing sugar.
■ All-purpose flour is plain household flour or white flour. When self-rising flour is used in place of all-purpose flour in a recipe that calls for leavening, omit the leavening agent (baking soda or baking powder) and salt.
■ Light corn syrup is golden syrup.
■ Cornstarch is cornflour.
■ Baking soda is bicarbonate of soda.
■ Vanilla is vanilla essence.

USEFUL EQUIVALENTS

⅛ teaspoon = 0.5ml
¼ teaspoon = 1ml
½ teaspoon = 2 ml
1 teaspoon = 5 ml
¼ cup = 2 fluid ounces = 50ml
⅓ cup = 3 fluid ounces = 75ml
½ cup = 4 fluid ounces = 125ml

⅔ cup = 5 fluid ounces = 150ml
¾ cup = 6 fluid ounces = 175ml
1 cup = 8 fluid ounces = 250ml
2 cups = 1 pint
2 pints = 1 litre
½ inch =1 centimetre
1 inch = 2 centimetres

BAKING PAN SIZES

American	Metric
8x1½-inch round baking pan	20x4-centimetre sandwich or cake tin
9x1½-inch round baking pan	23x3.5-centimetre sandwich or cake tin
11x7x1½-inch baking pan	28x18x4-centimetre baking pan
13x9x2-inch baking pan	32.5x23x5-centimetre baking pan
2-quart rectangular baking dish	30x19x5-centimetre baking pan
15x10x2-inch baking pan	38x25.5x2.5-centimetre baking pan (Swiss roll tin)
9-inch pie plate	22x4- or 23x4-centimetre pie plate
7- or 8-inch springform pan	18- or 20-centimetre springform or loose-bottom cake tin
9x5x3-inch loaf pan	23x13x6-centimetre or 2-pound narrow loaf pan or paté tin
1½-quart casserole	1.5-litre casserole
2-quart casserole	2-litre casserole

OVEN TEMPERATURE EQUIVALENTS

Fahrenheit Setting	Celsius Setting*	Gas Setting
300°F	150°C	Gas Mark 2
325°F	160°C	Gas Mark 3
350°F	180°C	Gas Mark 4
375°F	190°C	Gas Mark 5
400°F	200°C	Gas Mark 6
425°F	220°C	Gas Mark 7
450°F	230°C	Gas Mark 8
Broil		Grill

* Electric and gas ovens may be calibrated using Celsius. However, increase the Celsius setting 10 to 20 degrees when cooking above 160°C with an electric oven. For convection or forced-air ovens (gas or electric), lower the temperature setting 10°C when cooking at all heat levels.